M000288413

Miracles of the Heart
Looking Back on God's Pathway

by

Carol Eicher

DORRANCE
PUBLISHING CO
EST. 1920
PITTSBURGH, PENNSYLVANIA 15238

The contents of this work, including, but not limited to, the accuracy of events, people, and places depicted; opinions expressed; permission to use previously published materials included; and any advice given or actions advocated are solely the responsibility of the author, who assumes all liability for said work and indemnifies the publisher against any claims stemming from publication of the work.

All Rights Reserved
Copyright © 2021 by Carol Eicher

No part of this book may be reproduced or transmitted, downloaded, distributed, reverse engineered, or stored in or introduced into any information storage and retrieval system, in any form or by any means, including photocopying and recording, whether electronic or mechanical, now known or hereinafter invented without permission in writing from the publisher.

Dorrance Publishing Co
585 Alpha Drive
Pittsburgh, PA 15238
Visit our website at *www.dorrancebookstore.com*

ISBN: 978-1-6366-1172-3
eISBN: 978-1-6366-1763-3

Acknowledgments

Miracles of the Heart came about and developed into a book differently than the usual pathway to a book. Being an author of a book or books was not one of the desires of my heart in my younger life. I did not follow the usual pathway of writing a book, as I was not even aware of that pathway. However, as the miracles unfolded in my life, a desire to tell others about it was in my heart and soul. I started this book not long after Jack's heart transplant, just writing about the miracles and saving them on a flash drive. There was very little time to put these thoughts in order or write, as I was teaching high school full time and making regular trips back and forth between Kentucky and North Carolina. The heartbreaker was when my book flash drive was stolen from my car, along with my laptop computer. I had a rough draft, and I mean rough, on another flash drive. I did not write again for several years.

But the Lord was at work and kept me thinking. Even during that non-writing time, I had hints from the Lord to keep going. I would share one of the miracles in a Bible study group and someone would say, "You should write a book." Our pastor would have a message that just spoke to me to keep going. People that knew I had started a book would ask me, "How is that book coming?" I kept a tote bag with anything that might belong in my book—church bulletins with circled areas that spoke to me, handwritten notes from a sermon, Bible verses scribbled on scrap paper, books on writing a book, even had a calendar with a quote on it. However, there was no writing taking place. I even started a small embroidery business in my home, leaving little time for writing or even thoughts of writing.

There are special people to acknowledge in this unusual pathway to a book. At times, I would be carrying guilt because I was not writing and felt this a duty given to me by the Lord. As I voiced this guilt to a friend at church that already was a published author, she shared with me, "Books get written when they are supposed to." Well, that was a relief to hear. From then on, I still had the desire but not the guilt.

The day I retired from teaching high school in 2008, my friend and coworker, Mary King, said, "Maybe now you will have time to finish that book." Those words have strolled through my brain many times and helped to keep my dream alive.

During the past two years, there have been those who have spoken words that kicked up that desire to "finish that book." First to say thank you to would be Susan Park. Susan brought together a group of women to form the Christian Business Women's Leadership Networking Group. It is a group providing great encouragement to each other as we desire to be Christian leaders in our communities. Susan knew I was SLOWLY working on a book. She has such an uplifting, encouraging spirit, and a vision for others within her that anyone around her feels as if they can pursue their dreams. She already saw me as an author! If she thought I was an author, maybe I better finish that book so I could be an author.

Then there was that lunch with Lisa Hummel. I have known Lisa several years in our church. She is also in our Networking Group. One thing we do in the group is to have a one-on-one lunch with another member to see how we can support them in their business, ministry or nonprofit. That day I warned Lisa I wanted to talk "book." Her words were God chosen as she made suggestions as how I could manage my time to have writing time, spoke of the need for people to read about the miracles and gave other words of encouragement. However, the words that stuck deeply within me as we were finishing and I was rambling about waiting on God to get me going were "Maybe God is waiting on you." And then she smiled. As soon as I got home, I wrote those words down on a sticky note, dated it and taped it to my bathroom mirror. Those words were the ones that excited me to start writing again. That sticky note is still on my mirror. I believe it can apply to many things as we walk on the pathway God has for us. Thank you, Lisa, for the words God gave you to pass on to me.

Rose Sharon Hunt was so important in this journey to finish that book. She was the only one that read my manuscript. Besides being a long-time wonderful friend, she is an avid reader and is a certified teacher of English and Latin. Who better to read and evaluate this book? She read it when it was in pieces and not finished. I mainly wanted to know it was even something anybody would want to read. She gave me some great pointers and encouraged me to get it finished. I cannot thank her enough for that.

Of course, there is my amazing miracle man, Jack. He is the one that endured through all the medical problems, issues and pain. He is the one that most of the miracles were bestowed upon. He is the one that was healed repeatedly. He is the one that never lost faith while on God's pathway. To him, thank you for being such an example of faith in the toughest of days and loving me through it all.

Introduction

This is a story, a true story of two hearts. One heart that was terribly enlarged, depending on a pacemaker and defibrillator, just plain worn out and ready to give up, and another heart that wanted to keep on beating. It is a story about the miracles Jesus still performs today. It is a story about a plan for life in the hands of God on a pathway he planned oh, so long ago. It is a story about faith when times are tough, peace when times are rocky and vision when the great blessings come from God.

As many Bible stories reveal to us, God looks for ordinary people who are available to do his work. As the work is in progress and then done, God is glorified. It is my heart's desire for this miraculous story of an ordinary guy as told by an ordinary woman to bring glory to God, our awesome Father. Of course, the most available person in this story is the donor who was willing to give their heart to anyone who needed it.

It is my hope that this story will bring joy and blessings to those who read it. I also hope that this story gives the reader an ability to look back on his or her own life and see God's unique plan and pathway for each of them at work and recognize miracles all around them, especially if they are going through a season of troubles or turmoil.

"The invariable mark of wisdom is to see the miraculous in the common."
– Ralph Waldo Emerson

"Let us give thanks to God and the Father of our Lord Jesus Christ from whom all help comes! He helps us in all our troubles SO that WE are able to help others who have all kinds of troubles, using the same help that we ourselves have received from God…..We share in God's great help" (2 Cor 1:3-5, Good News Bible).

CHAPTER 1

The Donor Is Close, Very Close

"The donor is close, very close." Those words from the resident doctor flew quickly in my ears and sent my thoughts racing from one hospital to the next in the Charlotte area. Let's see, there's University Hospital, Presbyterian, and NorthEast. I was sure there were more that I didn't know since we hadn't been in the area long. The words roamed within my mind and then came to a sudden halt replaced by the huge realization: This is a miracle! Our precious donor's heart will not have to be flown many miles to save the life of my waiting husband. A Miracle! Could this be just one of the miracles that were about to be laid at my feet as we awaited one of the most amazing medical procedures of our day? Little did I know the many miracles before us.

What is it about the human heart that so intrigues and fascinates us as humans? What makes a heart transplant seem paramount to all other surgeries? Is it the many Biblical references to the heart? Is it the hundreds of poems written? The stories told and books written? The plays performed? The songs sung? The movies? The heart is awesome. We can't live without it. And we only have one. We feel it is such a part of our being—how we love, how we respond to others, how we feel joy, happiness, sadness, grief. But as the human anatomy goes, it is just a pump. A very efficient one but just a pump.

Let's begin this journey way back in 1969. On the eve of Jack's knee surgery in Lexington, Kentucky, I received a tearful phone call from him.

"Carol, the doctor has told me I can't play sports anymore. There is something wrong with my heart. A murmur or something. They discovered it on my pre-op examination. Can you come?"

My own heart felt like it sank to my feet, leaving a pit in my stomach as it went by. "Oh, no! I'll try to come but I'll have to borrow a car." As a student at WKU, I had no car. However, a great friend of mine did and she was very generous about sharing other things—stereo, clothes, food, etc. She said yes immediately when I told her the situation. I headed to Lexington, about a two-hour drive, early the next morning to find a very sad fiancé who felt his life had just been ripped from him. Sports, football and baseball, to be exact, were his life. He was a starting tackle for the Centre College Colonels football team and the starting catcher for the baseball team. He had loved sports since he was a little boy and had played at every opportunity. His knee surgery was to "fix" his knee so he would be ready to go come fall football practice. However, the Lord had other plans for the love of my life. Sometimes we arrange our life and God rearranges.

Thus began our journey towards an eventual heart transplant thirty-eight years down life's pathway. Our donor was not yet born when all this upheaval was happening. Jack's knee was repaired but this new heart problem prevented him from playing football or baseball as a senior at Centre College. Amazingly, Centre allowed Jack to be a student coach for both football and baseball his senior year. While it wasn't Jack's dream of how he would complete his college education, it was a great experience for a young man who would spend the bulk of his career coaching and molding the lives of high school boys.

CHAPTER 2

The Pathway from Kentucky to North Carolina
March 2007

"The donor is in THIS hospital," Jack said softly to me as I returned to his room after stepping out to make some phone calls. A doctor had come by to check on him and had told him that our donor had passed away right in the same hospital where the heart transplant would be performed. While thinking about the hospitals nearby, I hadn't even thought about THIS hospital. What a miracle that was! I thanked God immediately with my thoughts jumping to the donor's family. Not only was the donor in THIS hospital but his or her family probably was too. My heart went out to them with sympathy and overwhelming thankfulness.

One of the concerns for Jack in surgery would be what is called oozing from his sternum as he had had three previous open-heart surgeries and scar tissue was abundant. Apparently oozing is difficult to stop, making timing of the essence for the opening of the chest cavity. So now timing could be much more controlled than if the doctors were waiting for a heart to be flown in or even driven across town. As I found out later, the heart was simply walked across the hallway from the organ harvesting room to Jack's operating room.

It is an emotionally wrenching time while waiting for heart transplant surgery to begin. While great joy is within a person for the hope that lies before, there is great sadness for the donor's family. While recipients and their families may never meet the donor's family, the connection between families is immediate. Since I can only speak from the recipient side and for our family, I feel the bond is eternal. God links you forever. I never had such strong opposite feelings, one of joy and one of sadness, at the same time as I did during our time of waiting for the surgery to begin. I knew a family was grieving for their loved one. I wondered about the age of the donor, if they were married, had children, had great friends, a mom and dad, brothers and sisters—all those sorts of things.

So how did we get to Charlotte, NC, from our beloved Kentucky, the state I had lived in my entire life? Except for six years in California, Jack had always lived in Kentucky also. Jack had been under the care of the local university heart failure program for quite a while since his heart was underperforming after his 1998 surgery to replace the aortic valve for the second time. However, when it became apparent that Jack needed a transplant soon, the local transplant program was having some insurance coverage issues. Our insurance coordinator informed me that we could go anywhere in the country to await and receive the transplant. She told me how to check out the stats of all the heart transplant centers in the U.S. When I looked up Carolinas Medical Center stats, I got excited. We were planning to retire to the Charlotte area and had already built a house there to be closer to our two sons. Calling the heart transplant center on a Tuesday even made me more excited as they wanted us there for an interview with one of the doctors on Friday. Things were starting to happen. So, on Friday, we drove from London, Kentucky, to Charlotte, NC. While I was packing for this weekend trip, I made sure I had on the angel necklace my sister, Cheri, gave me after our mom passed in 1997. I wore it almost everywhere as it somehow connected me

4

to my mom and my sister. It also verified my belief that angels watch over us.

One of the things I did while writing this book was to go through emails I had copied to a flash drive. There was no Facebook yet. It was like reliving the three and a half months of our waiting for a heart and Jack's recovery after the transplant. From the time we started our heart journey until I quit sending regular updates by email, we lost three special people that have been in our lives for a long time. Our friend from London First Christian Church, Bill Huber, Jack's cousin by marriage, Nancy Flynn, and my sweet college roommate and Kappa Delta Big Sis, Harriet Rice Havron. All three died from some form of cancer. Harriet and Nancy answered every one of my emails while Jack waited and recovered. It has been a joy to read their words again, but so sad to know they are no longer on this earth to email or talk to or be with the spouses that wait to see them again in heaven. We have also had two friends lose grandsons at birth. Two friends have lost one of their parents. The passage of time and the circle of life continue in God's big plan.

One of the blessings, or I should say many blessings, that occurred during this time was the renewal of friendships that have beautiful histories of time gone by but physical distances that kept us apart. The pressures of time, distance and the commitment of raising children had taken its toll. It was so good to hear from those friends again. Some even came to see Jack as we waited. I can still feel the hugs from those precious friends that felt so good and full of love.

Other friends did whatever they could in London for us. Some watched our home, even went in every couple days to make sure all was well. At the time, I was a high school teacher of Family and Consumer Sciences at South Laurel High School in London. My wonderful friend, Rose Sharon Hunt, a retired Latin teacher, was substitute teaching at the time. She was so gracious to take the job as my sub, teaching Nutrition and Foods and Nutritional Science. Quite a different discipline from her beloved Latin. Even she claims it was a stretch for her! My coworkers in Family and Consumer Sciences, Mary King and Bethani

Carmichael, stepped up and helped in every way possible to cover my other school responsibilities. I did not give one moment of worry to how my classes were going during my absence. I knew they were in the best hands possible. God gives us Christian friends in our everyday life. In times of need, those friends seem like angels. I could not have asked for better angels than those three.

CHAPTER 3

The Interview and Testing - A Solid Step on the Pathway

Friday, December 8, 2006: As we drove up to Carolinas Medical Center for the interview, I was surprised to see a beautiful fountain in front. It gave me a feeling of peace and safety despite my deep fears. After negotiating our way to the hospital, the parking lot, and the hallways, we found our way to the right place in that very big hospital. We met Dr. Sanjeev Gulati, one of the doctors on the transplant team. He talked with us for about an hour and a half. I remember him asking me if Jack had always looked that greenish color. I did not think he had a green tint to him. Funny when you are with someone every day and they are gradually declining, you may not notice such things. I had a great feeling of security in THAT office with THAT doctor. He thought Jack was a possible candidate for a heart transplant. That was music to my ears, as the saying goes. But many tests would have to be done to confirm that good news.

Next Dr. Gulati asked us if we had a place to stay while they tested Jack the next week, which was planned start on Monday.

You should have seen his face when we said we owned a home in the area and could be close by if needed. What a pathway God had us walking on with Him! You see, we had built a house in the area two years before with thoughts of retiring there or selling it if we changed our minds. Both of our sons, Jeff and John, lived in the area. To have this life-ending health issue occur AFTER we built the house was surely the work of God leading us without us even knowing it. Where is God leading you? You may not be aware, as we were not aware at the time. However, this was just the beginning of the great opportunity we had to look back at the work of God leading our pathway as we walked a life of faith. Today we do not know the path that is before us, but God's path is still there. For us, our belief that God's plans are in action in each of our lives is much stronger than before we walked the transplant pathway. Today none of us know the path that is before us, but God knows.

It was after 5:00 P.M. when our interview was over but Dr. Gulati was not done with Jack. He said he wanted to get blood from Jack so they would have all the bloodwork done BEFORE he checked in the hospital for tests on Monday. He called a few places in the BIG hospital to see who was still open to take blood. He found one open. We quickly headed there and blood was taken from Jack. As we started towards our car, I felt like I was walking on a golden pathway. I said to Jack that I wasn't sure what it would take to get us here to wait for a heart but this was the place I wanted and we needed to be. This was the second of many impressive things that took place in that hospital. The first was the phone call there on Tuesday. Miracles were ahead. I could just feel it. Although we were just planning to stay the weekend at our future retirement house, the Lord had another schedule for us. But I then I remembered I had just brought clothes for the weekend. Funny the things that go through our mind at times.

Dec. 11, 2006: Monday was check-in day for Jack at the hospital for the tests to see if he truly was a candidate for a heart transplant. We were there and ready by 11:30 A.M., waiting to be called for the tests in a special heart waiting area that became a place of comfort for me as time continued. A catherization was done to measure pressures inside heart. He had had a few of those over the years. I think it is important to note that Jack never had blocked arteries or a heart attack. Although that is a common heart issue, it is only one of many. He also had an ultrasound on his organs and more blood tests. His medication was changed to prepare him for the wait time, which hopefully and prayerfully was ahead. He was checked into the hospital for a few days.

Dec. 12, 2006: On Tuesday a pic line was inserted and he was moved to a regular room, which was comforting as I could stay in there all the time. The pic line brought lifesaving meds to his weakened heart. During this testing time, we met Dr. Alan Thomley and Dr. Theodore Frank. They presented such a welcoming and knowledgeable feeling, it just solidified my feeling of this was where the Lord wanted us to be. Ever have that peace of yes, this is where I should be? The peace Jesus promised and delivers is beyond human explanation.

Dec. 13, 2006: Wednesday was a pulmonary test. And then an amazing thing happened. The transplant nurse that day was named Katie. She knew we were from Kentucky and immediately started talking about Kentucky stating she was from Louisville. Well, I could not have been happier at that moment. Someone from "home" to watch over Jack. Even though we had Jeff and John, our sons, near us in Charlotte, I still felt so far from my Kentucky home. And then came Katie. She was excited to see us as very few if any people come from Kentucky to get a heart transplant in Charlotte. Needless to say, we bonded immediately.

Dec. 14, 2006: Thurs.: This was the day we were anxiously waiting. Would Jack be a candidate for a heart transplant or not? Would we begin a waiting game or head home with little hope for Jack? Susan, one of the transplant nurses who we had met briefly at the original interview, appeared smiling at Jack's doorway. She pulled up a chair for the beginning of a detailed talk. First, she shared with us that Jack was a strong candidate for a transplant. I let out a very large sigh of relief. She went on to discuss all the pros and cons of the lifesaving surgery and described living with someone else's natural heart. The main possible dangers include rejection of the heart by the recipient's immune system and the heightened chance of infection or cancer due to a compromised immune system. The only negative from Jack's many tests was the condition of his kidneys. They were not fully functioning and in some cases, heart transplant patients with kidney issues need a kidney transplant in a few years as the anti-rejection meds are very hard on the kidneys. That didn't sound fun at all to me but certainly not a factor to say no to a chance to live longer. All the information and directions sounded doable to me. Of course, I wasn't the one to go through it. We each asked a few questions. Then Jack asked the big question: "How long do I have to live if I chose not to do this?" Susan looked him straight in the eyes and said, "Probably less than a year." He then said, "I'm ready to do this." He had made the decision to go through with surgery! She said he would probably be on the waiting list on Monday as that was the transplant team's weekly meeting day and we would be called. Monday! Four more days to wait to be on the waiting list! There are times in a Christian's life when you just plain know that God is with you and everything will be okay. That was one of those moments in time for me. I just knew. Have you had those times? He promises to always be with us. Those moments in human time are indescribable in human words.

That was the point in our lives where our cell phones became a part of our physical bodies. We were not going to miss any calls from this awesome team that was poised to save Jack's life, give him a second life, so to say. Jack was discharged and we headed to our house in Concord, a short 20 minutes away to wait for a call on Monday. We were assigned a home nurse who would check on Jack twice a week. Her name was also Susan. Seemed as if Susans were watching over us.

CHAPTER 4

Far Away from Home but Still on the Pathway

While we were far from our London home, our church in London was having an in-depth Bible study meeting every Thursday evening. Jack and I were a faithful part of that before we were aware Jack would need a heart transplant. What started as a Bible study became a support and prayer group for the two of us. Little did Jack and I know we would miss half of the classes because we would need to move to Charlotte, NC, to wait for a "fresh" heart and recover there. Every study session closed with the group standing in a circle, holding hands and praying for whatever needs were shared. We prayed for each other, people in our church, community and world. That was always special. A few weeks into the study, prayer began for Jack, as the need for a lifesaving heart transplant grew closer. Many people supported us in prayer as we waited and were on the pathway to our miracle. Every Thursday night after our move to Charlotte, we would think of our Bible study group and knew they were holding both of us up in prayer. That was such a blessing! Although I do not even remember which book of the Bible we were studying, the term "disciple" came alive in me, like a lightbulb with a dimmer switch getting brighter. Discipleship is about God's people. It is serving people, praying for people, loving people and trusting God for everything you need to serve all those people. I am so very thankful for our group which gave us much strength as Jack was given a second chance to be a husband, dad, brother, cousin, friend and most of all a Papa.

Prayers are simply amazing. Until you have had many people praying for you or your loved ones, praying that they would live and not die, "the power of prayer" is like a hidden mystery of the Lord. But when the prayers are for you the real "power" and the Lord's love are felt so deeply. Sometimes our prayer requests are not answered like we want or think they should be. That, of course, remains one of God's mysteries and is not in the realm of this book. However, I do believe the prayers of his children are heard, no matter how they are answered. The answer can be as we asked, delayed, given a bit at a time, differently than we expected or denied for reasons we do not know. I do want to say that praying for a transplant to come about is a prayer with mixed emotions as another person must pass before the perfect organ for a transplant recipient can become available. That other person is a much-loved family member to others. One that they will miss for the rest of their lives, struggling through birthdays, holidays or just everyday kind of days when grief overwhelms them. These thoughts and emotions are not lost on those praying for someone awaiting an organ transplant.

Dec. 15, 2006: Friday, we had our first visit from our home nurse, Susan. We chatted a bit to get to know each other, she changed the bandage or the pic line and flushed the pic line. Jack began to have some pain in his ankle and shoulder joints because of the medicine that was being sent to his heart through the pic line from the pack he wore around his waist. I referred to the pack as his fanny pack. He did not seem to find much humor in that term. The big question we asked Susan that first day was, "Can we drive back to London for the weekend to get some things we need from our home?" Remember, Jack and I only brought clothes for a weekend when we thought we were just coming for an interview. Our retirement home just had one bed in the master, one bed in the guestroom, one couch and one matching chair and a bistro-type table with four chairs. I had a minimum supply of kitchen equipment and now I would be cooking healthy meals. We needed some things as we did not know if the wait would be one week or months. I was also concerned about the classes I was teaching. It was near the end of the semester and we were on a block schedule so my classes would be over right before Christmas. I had notebooks to grade, final exams to prepare and final grades to figure. There was also the upcoming semester that I would miss some or maybe all my classes. Who would the administration hire to take my beloved job of teaching? So, we asked if we could please go to London before Jack was on the list. Amazingly, Susan said yes, we could go.

Dec. 16, 2006: On Saturday we got up early and drove six hours to Kentucky in order to prepare for an unknown length of time and stay in NC. As soon as we arrived, Jack started to gather what he thought we needed to take back. I immediately drove to school and worked six hours straight. Since it was a Saturday, the only other person there was our security guard. He would poke his head in my classroom door to see how I was doing. It was such a comfort to know he was looking out for my safety. The bulk of my time was evaluating TIP notebooks. My TIP students had captured a special corner of my heart. TIP stood for "Teachers In Preparation." They were senior high school students interested in any type of career in education. They were more focused on college and career than any other students I had the joy of teaching. It was so rewarding to see the "teacher hearts" in each of them begin to gain and develop skills needed to teach. They each had a class notebook to turn in as a part of the final grade for the class. It was a mighty task to get them all graded in one day. But they each deserved my time. My present status in life had nothing to do with the lives of these future teachers. So grade I did and I did finish, leaving each with a prayer that their dream of becoming a teacher, principal, school psychologist, or counselor would come true. I have followed many of my students from that class and my following TIP classes. Many are outstanding teachers affecting not only the lives of their students but the lives of future generations. I obviously have not been able to keep up with all of them but loved each one of them.

Besides the TIP notebooks, I had exams to have ready to go to end the semester. I also had a Nutritional Science class starting in January. I made sure my unit map was ready to go for whoever might be teaching that class, one filled with science concepts, experiments and food labs. After a long Saturday, I headed to our London home and crashed in the bed. Sunday found us up early, packing what was needed for what could be a very long stay in Charlotte. It was hard trying to decide what to take and what to leave behind. Jack could not pack much as he was weak and quickly became short of breath. But we carried on and packed our car as tightly as possible. But we could not leave without going to our church.

Sunday morning at our London church was a family ritual for us. One that our week seemed incomplete if we missed it. People were so glad to see us. It was good to be home if just for a bit of heartwarming time. The church we were a part of did not practice the laying on of hands for healing or praying. Near the end of the service, the minister acknowledged that was not a usual practice of that church but felt a calling to do so for Jack and me. He invited those that wanted to come forward. I wasn't quite sure about this. I had laid hands on others to pray for them but had not had it done to me. We moved to the front pew as asked as the minster moved from the pulpit towards us. And then surprisingly, others joined all around us putting their hands on us. What an overwhelming feeling of love, hope and healing in the future for us. I so distinctly remember my friend, Patty, sat next to me and took my hand in hers. It was so comforting to me. It seemed she represented my women's circle that had meant so much to me over the years. The minister prayed over us. I do not remember one word of that prayer but can still feel the warmth and love of those hands on my shoulders and head and the tears flowing down my cheeks. I knew I could face whatever was ahead, be it healing of Jack through a transplant or the loss of my precious Jack. Sometimes Jesus is so present, you are sure if you open your eyes, he will be physically right in front of you. So you just keep those eyes closed. That is how it was that day in that church that had been so important in our lives. After that wonderful experience, we headed to our car and drove to Charlotte for what we hoped would be a wait for a heart transplant. As we settled in, Jack and I both felt the Spirit of God with us.

"Peace I leave with you; my peace I give to you. Not as the world gives do I give to you. Let not your hearts be troubled; neither let them be afraid" (John 14:27, English Standard Version).

CHAPTER 5

Waiting on the Pathway

Dec. 18, 2006: Monday, was the day we would get the call to let us know if Jack had made the list for possible transplant recipients. We did not know what time the team met so we did not know when the call would come. I can no longer remember what time the anticipated call came. But it did come with the great news we and others had prayed for. Jack had joined the list of many people needing a heart transplant. There was solid hope for the future. Now the real wait was beginning. We were in waiting mode, hoping for a short wait time until THE CALL, just like anyone else on an organ transplant wait list. We knew if we did not get THE CALL in about nine months to a year, Jack's earthly life would end. So, we put our trust in the Lord, and tried to wait patiently.

Waiting on the Lord brings the development of patience and deeper faith. Have you ever waited on the Lord? Most of us have. I believe the hard part of waiting on the Lord is not knowing God's will for the outcome. Fear creeps in when we think that God's plan is not what we are praying to happen. That is where the faith grows and deepens. We pray for what we want but give it to God and his plan without fear.

"For God gave us a spirit not of fear, but of power, love and self-control" (2 Timothy 1:7, ESV).

The following verse comes to mind when I think of the waiting period: **"But those who trust in the Lord for help will find their strength renewed. They will rise on wings like eagles, they will run and not get weary, they will walk and not get weak" (Isaiah 40:31, GNB).** This encouraging verse was the theme for the 1985 National Fellowship of Christian Athletes Camp at the Blue Ridge Assembly in Black Mountain, NC. I am not sure that I had ever heard the verse before I attended that camp with Jack. It became internalized within me from that week forward. Once again, the Lord gives light to our pathway in many ways but his Word is ever applicable to our daily lives. He had lighted our pathway on this earth with this verse in his Word 22 years earlier. Has he given you a verse or verses to light your pathway? Give that some thought. Are there verses you learned as a child or young adult or just last week that the Holy Spirit brings to your mind when you need them most? Maybe it is for you or maybe it is to be shared with someone who needs it. If you have some favorites, I recommend you write them down somewhere or store them in a device.

Our life was totally different from what we had left behind in Kentucky. I was teaching full time and Jack had retired from education and coaching, was a real estate agent and working our landscaping business. We went from being away from each other for most of the day to being together constantly. We had almost no responsibilities as all that we were doing in Kentucky was now being covered by much loved friends. My thoughts were often focused on what I had left behind at school: a hectic schedule with each school day crammed full with working with students, interacting with coworkers and friends, fulfilling the obligations of a high school teacher. My wonderful friend, Rose Sharon Hunt, checked on us almost every day. Even though I was miles away, I still felt connected.

When Laurel County had a snow day with no school, I was sure if I looked out my window, there would be snow on the ground in Charlotte too. Some days I would even sleep later. Our brains can do amazing things with time and place. We had to stay within a one hour drive from the hospital in case we got THE CALL. We had our cell phones literally on our bodies or right next to us at all times because if you miss THE CALL and do not respond in a certain amount of time, the heart goes to the next closest match awaiting their call. Those weeks were precious time together. Although Jack tired quickly, he felt fairly well due to the medicine being pumped through his pic line. We had relaxing mornings without the hustle bustle to get out the door for the day's work. We were not very familiar with the Charlotte area so if Jack felt good enough, we would go places within one hour's time to explore. Sort of like we were on a leash. We would find some place new to eat lunch and then head back home for him to rest. Prayers were being said by both of us throughout the day. You know the verse "Pray without ceasing." Well, that was me. Family and friends would call every day to check on Jack and even me. It was great to be physically close to our sons, daughter-in-law and twin grandsons. It was a precious time. A time when I knew time together could be over soon or life could go on miraculously with a heart from someone else. Deep down, I continually had faith that he would receive a heart. He felt the same but was well prepared mentally and spiritually if God had another plan. As an act of faith, we added a small sunroom/back porch to our house. We had planned to add it at some point after moving into the house. We had faith that God's intricate plan had brought us to Charlotte, faith that Jack would receive a fresh heart, and faith we were going to be on earth to enjoy our little porch for a long time. And we have. Faith can show itself in so many ways. Our faith is like a shield from all the "maybes" that we envision can happen. **Ephesians 6:16 says to carry faith as a shield, a part of the armor God has given us, AT ALL TIMES so we can be able to put out the burning arrows shot by the Evil One (GNB).** You know those burning arrows. Doubt that God is with you, doubt that he will answer your prayers, doubt that you are living his will for you and on and on and on. Faith is one of the spiritual gifts of the

Holy Spirit. **"One and the same spirit gives faith to one person
…" (I Corinthians 12:9, GNB).** So embrace your faith. Hold it
up as a shield to protect you and walk the pathway God has for you.
Susan, one of the transplant nurses, commented after the surgery
and some recovery time that Jack and I seemed calmer and more
matter of fact about the entire heart transplant experience than most
other patients and their families. I do believe that was a sign of our
faith in God's plan for our lives.

Do you have faith in God's plan for your life? How does faith
look in your life? Or is there faith in your life? Have you had
some challenging times and your faith was there but you were
not aware it was a gift from the Holy Spirit? Or have there been
great times or just everyday times and your faith was there, but
you were unaware? I would recommend becoming more aware
of your faith, the belief in the unseen, the ability to trust God with
full confidence that He is in charge. It is a way to worship God
and be aware of his constant presence with each of us.

What would Christmas be like this year? We had always been
together at some time during the holidays. Could we make it
happen this year? Jack and I were tied to the Charlotte area. The
boys were close by so that was good news for them. But what
about our daughter, Emily, her husband, Herb, and grandson
Joseph? Could they make it to Charlotte to celebrate Christmas
with us? These were thoughts and questions flying through my
head as the holiday season got closer. We had all planned to be in
London as always before all the transplant movements began to
happen. Now what? No one could help but think this might be
our last Christmas with Jack. While I have always believed in
miracles and truly believed Jack would be the recipient of one,
human thoughts, perhaps of the devil, still invade our human
minds and give us reasons to doubt that God will provide us with
what we ask. Also, even the most devout of Christians know God
doesn't answer all our prayers for miracles in the way we ask in
the lives of those we love. Of course, that mystery is another
entire book. What we do know as Christians is that God will be
with us for comfort and strength whatever comes our way and
whatever the outcome.

Joyfully, we did all get together at our home in Concord. I should know better than to doubt Emily's ability to pull off any event or activity that deems itself in the best interest of the family. She is an amazing organizer and will go above and beyond the expected to accomplish that which she sees as important. And our boys, Jeff and John, would be there whenever needed. Not only were we together for a joyous and blessed Christmas, but we managed to have a neighbor take a family picture of us that day and I sent out "Happy New Year" cards as there was no time for Christmas cards that year. The twins and their cousin were together. Getting the grandsons together has always been and still is a strong desire of Jack's heart. I think that comes from his great memories of his four cousins from Illinois. We remain close to them, despite the many miles between us. The blessings continued in our newfound home in the simple sharing of meals, watching the boys together, our adult children, which includes our in-law children talking and sharing. It all seems sweeter when in the throes of tough times. One of the miracles of tough times is the ability to see everyday events in a new light and appreciation. Maybe God allows our eyes to see things as He does during those times. I developed my definition of being wise early in my adult life at some Bible study of which I can't pinpoint right now. I believe wisdom is to see things as God sees them. As we draw closer to God and rely more on Him during tough times, perhaps he allows us this awesome ability to see things as He does. And so it was on that Christmas of 2006. Every little thing seemed special and I thanked God for that from the depths of my heart.

As I look back, that waiting time gave us some of our very best days together, totally focused on each other. Another example of how God can take the scariest of times and make them the best. Amazingly, we never had to go back to the transplant doctor for any issues except a quick checkup. The home nurse came two times a week and that proved to be enough. I kept remembering Dr. Gulati's words upon checking Jack out of the hospital after his four days of testing: "I hope the next time I see you is when you come back in for your fresh heart." And those proved to be true words. All part of the plan.

Below is our email version of a Christmas card that December in 2006. It went to many friends and extended family members.

From: Jack & Carol Eicher
Sent: Sunday, December 24, 2006 8:47 A.M.

Merry Christmas to all and A Happy New Year! For some of you, Christmas will be over by the time you read this. We wish for each of you and your family a Very Blessed Christmas!

We just wanted to let all of you know how much we appreciate all your thoughts, prayers and concerns about us. Since Christmas cards did not go out from the Eichers this year due to the many changes in our lives during the last two weeks, we wanted to let those in our email contacts list know that Jack is doing well. For those of you who do not know, we are presently living in Concord, NC while Jack waits for a heart transplant. The Lord is at work as our boys live here and we already owned a home here. We see the twins almost everyday! We have a peace and faith that all will go well.

With love to all,
Carol & Jack

An answer from our high school friends that are wonderful lifetime friends.

Carol and Jack,
Marcia and I were unaware of the need for a heart transplant. We will be out of town through New

Years. We would like to call you when we return to see if we could visit for a few hours. We don't want to burden you and if the time is not right we completely understand. We will keep you both in our prayers.

Love,
Carl & Marcia Falk

Dec. 29, 2006: We had an appointment with Dr. Gulati, the doctor we met with for the first interview. He declared Jack was doing well and would see us in three months with the hope that Jack would have a new heart before then and we could break that appointment. That sounded like great news to me.

Jan. 24, 2007: Jack started having pain in one of his teeth. We went to Jeff's dentist and were told Jack needed a root canal and they would start on it in a week. Well, that was not going to work! A patient undergoing surgery to receive a heart transplant cannot have ANY sign of infection in their body. That includes any dental problems. Well, what did this mean? If a match was found for Jack, he would be turned down for that heart, and it would go to the next person on the list. I was not going to let that happen. Not when Jack had 9-12 months to live. I immediately explained that to the scheduling person and guess what, she found another time much sooner. We can find strength deep down when it concerns the health and welfare of our loved ones. He completed the root canal before THE CALL for which I was very grateful.

Feb. 22, 2007: Jack's blood was too thick, as the non-medical laymen say. Our home nurse, Susan, would test it often and the doctors would make an adjustment to his meds and then test it again in a couple days. No big deal. Jack had "thinned" blood since 1973 to prevent a blood clot forming on his artificial aortic valve. This adjusting was nothing new to us.

It was about this time I was beginning to get a bit irritated with God and His time schedule. What was He waiting on? My planned waiting time was about up. Three months was the average wait time at Carolinas Medical Center and my sick days saved from teaching all those years would soon be used up. I had several conversations with God about this time issue with no resolution or word from Him, leaving me just plain irritable. Have you ever been irritated with the Lord? It is not a fun place to be. It fills a Christian with guilt. But sometimes it happens.

March 1, 2007: Jack's blood was still too "thick" and the doctors said they could not give him any more meds for it. This "thick" blood diagnosis had been given about two weeks prior. What is the world was going on here? Why wasn't the medicine working? While I worried over the possibility of a blood clot forming on the artificial valve, God was working on a miracle. Blind to our human eyes, God had a plan and was putting it into place. God is always at work!

CHAPTER 6

THE CALL – A Big Giant Step on the Pathway

Mar. 2, 2007, Friday: Jeff and Kim's three-year-old twins, Jackson and Jesse, were scheduled to spend the night with us. We had plans on Saturday for an Eicher Adventure Day which included fun activities at Latta Plantation. For some reason on that Friday night, I turned all that I had tried to carry myself the past couple weeks back over to God. I gave up my human fight of trying to get God to work from my timetable. I was instantly overwhelmed with a feeling of peace and suddenly felt more lighthearted than I had in a couple weeks. We can find many examples of obedience following human whining in the Bible. At our point of obedience, God performs the miracle. One example of that is Moses at the burning bush (Exodus 4:3-5). He is whining and is giving God his third excuse as to why he can't lead the people of Israel out of Egypt. God changed his walking stick into a snake, scaring Moses. Then the Lord commanded him to pick the snake up by the tail, not the safest way to pick up a snake. Moses obeyed and the second he touched the tail of the snake, God turned it back to a walking stick. When we obey God, and quit fighting him, that is when the miracles can occur. **"Let us hold fast the confession of our hope without wavering, for He who promised is faithful" (Hebrews 10:23, ESV).**

I found myself thinking how fun the next day was going to be, sharing the Eicher Adventure Day with the twins, Jeff and Kim. The twins landed at our house early in the evening in their usual fashion, fired up and ready to play. We had a fun evening with them. It was a joy to no longer be burdened with my time schedule I had expected God to follow. If my sick days ran out, the Lord would take care of us. He had held us together through many tight financial days when we were younger.

March 3, 2007: One thing Jack and I had tried to maintain during this wait time was consistent rest. We both wanted to feel rested whenever THE CALL came. Well, the twins were both up several times during the night and up early. I heard the scurry of feet come into my room about 6:00 A.M., a sound familiar to all parents. As I opened my eyes, there were those four beautiful eyes gazing into mine with two big smiles and someone asking when we would be leaving for Latta Plantation. So up I got, the first day since THE WAIT started that I had awakened tired.

Mar. 3, 2007: As I fixed breakfast for the twins, Jesse looked out the back door window and stated, "It's going to be a great day, Gammy." Out of the mouth of babes, as the saying goes. To this day, I believe those were words spoken by God through the sweet voice of a little boy. Over the years I have been in awe of God's voice speaking to me through another human. Often, I did not make the connection until later after an event or happening. Then I would have an ahha moment and know without a doubt He had spoken. Ever been there? When it happens, it makes my heart and spirit smile and say thank you to God.

The weather was great that day. Latta Plantation is a restored working plantation in Huntersville, NC, a bit north of Charlotte. It was our first visit there. The twins were interested in checking out the animals while Jack and I were interested in touring the plantation house. We split from them and headed toward the plantation house for the tour. First floor was very interesting. We headed upstairs and went in the first room. As the tour guide was speaking about the bedroom we were in, my phone rang at exactly 3:20. Since Jack had been put on the waiting list, both of us kept our cell phones on our bodies, as time is of the essence once a suitable heart match is found. I quickly stepped out of the room without looking at the incoming number.

"Hello?" I said.

"Hi. This is Katie with the Transplant Team. Are you ready for a big day?"

"Yes," I replied with the beginnings of trembling in my voice.

"We have a heart for Jack."

My own heartrate doubled.

"Is Jack with you?"

"Yes," I replied with an extremely trembling voice.

"May I speak with him?"

"Of course," I answered with an entire trembling body.

I stepped back to the door to get Jack's attention. He was on the other side of the room almost blocked from my view by the other people on the tour. I waved my hand and he looked at me like, why are you being so disruptive, and sort of shook his head. You know that head shake, just a little back and forth motion with a frown on the forehead and lips. It says stop whatever you are doing. You probably got it from your mom a few times while growing up. Then I proceeded to give the universal phone gesture learned from my daughter in her teen years: little finger to the mouth and thumb to the ear. I very clearly mouthed: "It's THE CALL!" while holding up the phone with my other hand. The frown instantly shifted to a look of shock and he quickly stepped out into the hall. While I paced within hearing distance, Katie gave him directions of where to go upon arrival at the hospital and how much time we had to get there. His voice was trembling as he spoke and then he gave the phone back to me. With both bodies shaking we briefly hugged, ran down the steps quickly, and exited the plantation house through the old weathered front door. As I think back, I wonder how many others had passed through that old weathered door at life-changing events in their lives.

Announcements of births or deaths, leaving home to go off to war or coming home after long travels. I have my doubts that there was anyone else who passed through that old weathered door to go get a heart transplant.

Where was Jeff? We looked around the yard area, walking around the house and yelling his name, but not having any idea how big the plantation was or where they could be. I called on his phone but he didn't answer. So I called again. This time he answered and I must have sounded irritated as I said, "Where are you?" in my excited voice. He answered, "I'm just a little way behind the house." It was that tone of voice that says, "Why are you talking to me like that?" When I told him they had a heart for Jack, he said, "I'll be right there," and showed up with rest of his family in a few seconds. I had always envisioned we were get the call while at our house. I knew just how to get to the hospital from our house. But from Latta Plantation, I didn't have a clue. Hadn't even paid attention as we drove there as we just followed Jeff. We hadn't purchased a GPS yet. It was decided I would drive straight to the hospital and Jack could call John and Emily on the way. Jeff and Kim would take the boys to the sitter and then come to the hospital. All six of us practically ran back through the entrance. I handed the laminated map back to the lady at the desk and said, "We are leaving for a heart transplant." She squealed as if she had known us for years and wished us luck. Jeff followed us to the car, knowing full well that the directions had not seeped into my directional being. He stood by the window and repeated them to me, slowly and deliberately, gave me a hug and backed off from the window of the car. I slowly backed up, put the car in drive and took off, I can still hear the sound of the wheels against the rocks in the parking lot as we pulled onto the road and turned right.

So here we were, driving to the hospital for our long-awaited miracle gift from an unknown generous person. Even in my excitement for Jack's surgery, my thoughts turned to the family that was grieving. What had happened to their loved one? Who was grieving? A wife? A husband? Small children? A mother or dad? It is one of God's miracles that in the making of man that we can have such a range of emotions. And that Jesus was capable of feeling all those emotions we feel today. I must admit that I had never felt emotions like this. My insides were shaking which was coming to the outside of me. I knew I had to get control of the shaking and concentrate on the driving task at hand. In times of emotional overload, the only thing I know to do is to call upon the Lord to bring things into control. I quickly sent up a prayer for the Lord to calm me and help me get Jack safely to the hospital. I felt a calm come over me immediately. I wasn't my normal self but at least I could think clearly and drive safely. The plan was for Jack to call Emily and John and let them know a heart had been donated that would fit and work for Jack. When we drove to a location where we knew the way to the hospital, Jack called them. His voice was shaking and tears filled his eyes as he gave the news to both of them. I was not sure he could get the words out as he was so choked up. He said that I would call them later with more details after we got checked in. Even though I had walked almost each step with Jack, I could not feel what he was feeling. There's that emotion thing again. Jack is a strong, but quiet person, living his Christian life by example. He rarely shares emotions with others. But taking out your heart and replacing it with a stranger's goes to the depth of your being. All I could do for him was be there and pray.

We made it safely to Carolinas Medical Center and as we turned right to head up the slight hill to the front door, there was that beautiful big fountain, the water sparkling as the sun shone on it giving it a heavenly look. I remembered that fountain affecting me before. The first time I saw it, I thought this looks like an entrance to a hotel, not a hospital. I have always loved moving waters, especially waterfalls. It sets the welcoming tone for the warmth of the staff that works there. Today it welcomed me back and gave me the feeling that everything was going to be okay. Up to the front door I drove as instructed by Nurse Katie. There is always a person outside of the front door to greet and give the first caring step from the hospital staff. There she was, a staff member of the "Guest Services" greeting me. I had calmed down to drive and thought I was all under control. However, when I jumped from the driver's side of the car, ran around to her and tried to say my husband is here for a heart transplant, no words would come from my mouth. I tried again, but no words. Finally, I was able to get out "My husband is here for a" and that was it. When I tried to say heart, nothing came out but air with a bit of an h sound. I tried again with no success. Of course, she was expecting us and figured out what I was saying. She smiled and seemed so excited. She grabbed a wheelchair, Jack got out of the car, turned and sat in it. She gave Jack some words of encouragement and then gave me instructions where to park and where to go in the hospital. Off they went, through the doors and I was on my own. I had been there before under less stressful situations and knew how to get to the parking garage. How could there be so many cars here today and why can't I find a spot? Finally, I pulled into one and headed to the 6th floor of the hospital. Another place I was more than familiar with the hallways and elevators. Although I knew the way, it seemed to take forever especially with all that shaking going on inside of me. The Lord had calmed me for the drive, but the shaking had returned. Finally, I was there!

I stopped by the nurses' station and identified myself as Jack Eicher's wife. One of the nurses gave me a big smile and escorted me right to his room rather than just giving me a room number. I guess they are familiar with the interior shaking and giving help whenever possible. There he sat in the bed with a huge grin on his face. His first words were "Guess who is getting me ready for all of this?" Before I could guess or ask who, he blurted out, "Nurse Cory!" And then she walked into the room. Now Cory held a special place in our hearts. Two years before, Jack had gone to the Charlotte NASCAR race by himself and passed out in a rocky parking lot due to a tachycardia attack. He ended up at Carolinas Medical Center and had a pacemaker with a defibrillator inserted. Cory was one of his caring nurses. One morning, Cory was late making her rounds and getting to Jack. She apologized and said she had been busy preparing a patient to receive a heart transplant. She seemed so excited about it. That was the first time I knew that CMC did heart transplants. Little did I know our future health would be there. So how cool was that – Cory would be preparing my Jack for his life saving surgery. I remembered her enthusiasm that day in 2005 and suddenly felt more at ease and more hopeful than I had since getting the news from Katie. I just felt at peace about what lay ahead of us. Funny how God places people in our lives to do His work. They just appear to be people going about their everyday lives doing their jobs and yet there they are for you at moments when you need them most. Take a few minutes to think about some of your past life situations. Who are the people that God has sent to you just at the right moment, just when you needed them most? So often our human side doesn't connect these people who are part of the big plan that God has for our life. Or that they are the "peace" God and Jesus promised so much in scripture. But if we rely more on the spirit side of our being, we can see it and even feel it. Sometimes we must go through the situation and look back and then we see the connection and the blessed gift. These are times to thank God for His actions in our life and realize we are walking through God's plan for our life. But too often, we just move right on to the next thing, not seeing God's hand in what has happened or who was sent to us. Busyness consumes us, leaving no time for reflection, connection to God or time to say thank you. How sad that must make our Heavenly Father as He created us to have a relationship with Him. Take time to look, see, be aware and be thankful of these times. The Father will bless your gratefulness. **Be thankful in all circumstances. This is what God wants from you in your life with Christ Jesus" (I Thessalonians 5:18, GNB).**

CHAPTER 7

The Surgery – Surrounded by Miracles on the Pathway

Since we were told to be at the hospital within an hour of the call that a heart had been found and I knew a heart had to be beating and giving life in its recipient four to six hours after death, I just assumed things would move along quickly. Oh, how much we learn in new situations. Now it is important to know that very little is revealed about the generous donor, only that the heart is a match and is being donated. Soon after I arrived, a resident doctor came and spoke with us. He said the donor was braindead and on life support to keep the heart beating. That meant the four-to-six-hour factor was out the window. The young resident doctor also said the donor was very close and the surgery would not begin until in the evening. "The donor was very close." Those words stuck in my ears. "Close." I wondered what that meant. Let's see, in the Charlotte area, I knew there were several major hospitals: University Hospital, Presbyterian Hospital and NorthEast. There could be more hospitals closer by that I didn't know about and how close is "close"? Where was our donor and that precious heart? Where was his or her grieving family? One thing I did figure out was that the heart probably would not need to be flown to the hospital. For Jack's situation that was another miracle in the making. Remember the "too thick" blood I wrote about? Well, seems God must have had a hand in that condition. Jack's blood was just thick enough for the surgery to take place! Therefore, no meds were needed to "thicken" it up. We already had an underlying miracle just a couple weeks ago. Although we were unaware of the transplant date, God had it pinned down exactly. Can you pinpoint some underlying miracles that led to the big miracles in your life? I feel sure you can think of at least one. You see, God is always at work. We as humans are not able to see it. Just know His work is for the good of his children. **"But He answered them, My Father is working until now, and I am working"** (John 5:17, ESV).

As we waited and nurses attended to Jack, I started calling family and friends to alert them and request prayer. How did we exist before cell phones? Our Emily had just arrived with her husband and young son in Nashville for a gathering with her husband's family. They had driven several hours from their home in Cape Girardeau, Missouri. She wanted to start towards her dad right away. I encouraged her to wait until morning as it was about a ten-to-eleven-hour drive and they would be driving through the night with a small child. She reluctantly agreed. Jeff and Kim had planned ahead of time to take the boys to their sitter's house and come to the hospital. They were putting the plan into action. Now John's schedule was part of the miracles that would open before our eyes. He was a member of a NASCAR pit crew and traveled every weekend there was a race. There are very few weekends once the season starts that there isn't a race. However, this weekend was "open" so he was in Charlotte with nowhere to go, so to speak. God's timing is humanly unbelievable and often part of a miracle itself. We try to plan our time and happenings for our advantage but things don't always go along with our timetable. I had an awesome adult Sunday School teacher, Jackie Thompson, that often would quote, "We arrange, then God rearranges." There really is A PLAN!

I'll never know all the calls that were made or emails that were sent that evening for prayers for Jack and me, but it seemed everyone knew. We had lived in four different towns in Kentucky and still had connections in all of them. There were a few people I called and then they called others. Therefore, I knew Jack was being held up to the Lord in prayer from many places. Praying across the miles is a human activity resulting in a phenomenon supported by scripture and enforced through the name of Jesus. Take, for instance, the following happening. Dear friends from our college and early married days, Mark and Julie Dexter, were hosting a small group of Christians in Danville that evening for a time of fellowship, sharing and, of course, food. Consider the following background information that the first two years after we were married, Jack and I lived in Danville where Jack was an assistant football coach, the wrestling coach and a science teacher. We absolutely loved it there. Life seemed simple then and we were so happy to be married after five and one half years of dating and waiting to complete college. One of our joys there was to be part of a "sharing" group. We would come together weekly at different members' homes, participate in Bible study, discussion and then pray for needs of the group. It was an essential part of my spiritual growth as a young married woman. So here is the miracle of the meeting at Mark and Julie's that night: All the people that were there that night had at one time or another been in our sharing group or had known us in Danville. One was even a professor of Jack's in college. That was 34 years ago! Julie was one of the people getting a call about Jack's surgery. What a miracle! Praying Christians that we knew well in Danville 36 years ago would be together in one place on the eve of Jack's surgery and pray for Jack and me as we awaited an uncertain future. **"For where two or three are gathered in my name, there I am among them" (Matthew 18:20, ESV).** Praying across the miles is not to be taken lightly. God brings people together in His time and His place and connects with them through prayer. How His ear must be tuned in when numbers of Christians pray for the same outcome, happening, healing, or people. While I have always believed in praying across the miles, this gathering put a new depth and reality on it for me. God is the great jigsaw puzzle solver and never fails to amaze by the way the pieces of life fit together.

With what looked like a long wait until surgery would begin and an all-nighter ahead, I knew I had to eat. I'm not a person that can go hours without food. I have hypoglycemia (low blood sugar) and getting very hungry does not make for a happy Carol. With lowered blood sugar, it is difficult to think clearly, not to mention make proper decisions. I've even been known to undergo a temporary personality change with a short fuse, so to speak. This was not the day to skip supper. Also, there was much for the nurses to do to Jack to prepare him for surgery. With this in mind, Jack insisted I head down to the hospital cafeteria to get some food. Off I went remembering the way from our stay there in 2005. A slice of cheese pizza with a Caesar salad with a Coke had become my comfort meal from our previous time there. I ordered it right up and sat down to eat. I was fueled up for the night ahead. Upon returning to Jack's room, I found I had missed a doctor telling him that our donor had passed away in Carolinas Medical Center. How crazy I felt—hadn't even considered that the donor could be right in the same hospital. As we pondered this new information, it became clear that the heart would just have to be carried across the hall. Not travel by air or ambulance, just walked across the hall. Wow! How could God be blessing us with such unusual circumstances? I have no idea what the data reveals about organs being harvested from donors and implanted in recipients in the same transplant center, but it just seems that it can't be a large number of organs. All I know is that I felt overwhelmingly blessed and felt that our family was the only family God was concerned with that night. You know, that is one of the characteristics of God we humans cannot understand. As Grady Nutt once stated, "God loves you as if you are the only person in the world and he loves each one of us just that much." Then my thoughts went to our donor's family. God was concerned with that family for sure on that night. Did I pass them in the hall earlier? Did Jack go by them as he was being wheeled in? Were they at their home already? Were there children who had just lost a mom or dad? What about parents? How their hearts must be aching for the one they had just lost.

The evening wore on with no dinner for Jack, of course. My thoughts kept going to Emily. I really missed having her with me. A mother-and-daughter bond is almost unexplainable. I knew how much she wanted to be there but distance was the great divider right now. I kept calling her to keep her posted but I really needed a hug from her. Jack's vitals continued to be taken after the prep work was complete. The resident doctor would come in once in a while and check on Jack, sharing some nonrelevant conversation. Then it happened. Dr. Mark Reames, the surgeon, walked in looking as if he had just marched out of military ranks, ready for battle. The game face was on. We had not met the surgeon yet as no one on the team knows which of the surgeons will be on call for the transplant. We knew names but no faces. He introduced himself, checked Jack over and said, "Looks like you and I will be spending the night together." Then he discussed with us the possible problem during surgery with Jack oozing blood at the chest opening due to the fact that this would be the 4th time his chest had been opened. Oozing blood is more difficult to stop than a bleeding artery as it cannot be clamped off. Oozing occurs in scar tissue and Jack had lots of that where the incision would be made. With game face on and discussing the possible bleeding issue, my own heart sank suddenly and I felt a deep fear. I had felt so hopeful, nervous, but hopeful up to this point. Knowing the heart was in the same hospital had been comforting but now this issue. The doctor shook Jack's hand, said something like see you soon, turned and walked away. My demeanor had changed so dramatically that I felt the need for reassurance. I followed him right out the door and stopped him in the hallway. My question was, "Is there hope?" Dr. Reames, still with his game face on, looked at me and said, "Of course there is hope. I must share the risks with the patient and family."

As I watched him walk down the hallway, I took a deep breath, sighed and my eyes focused on his hands. Oh, those hands, a gift from God that had saved many lives with heart transplants before Jack came along. I said a quick prayer for him and his medical staff which would be saving the life of my beloved Jack in the next few hours. I would not see Dr. Reames again until after the lengthy surgery.

About 10:00 P.M., someone from Guest Services, the dedicated team at CMS that transports patients from place to place in the hospital, came to take Jack to another place, the surgery floor. I can still remember the last-minute hustle of the nurses, making sure all was in place for the rolling bed trip to take Jack to the next step in the procedure toward the transplant surgery. Guest Services people were always friendly, lending a soothing sense to whatever was ahead. He and I chatted, our sons and daughter-in-law following, as we moved along what seemed like an endless pathway—down the hall, the elevator ride and another walk down a hall. Jack said very little as he had already had his first sedation shot and was very relaxed. And yet, what could be going through his mind? I knew he was in deep thought. A wife can tell these things after 30-something years of marriage and all that life requires over that time. I could not imagine his thoughts during this time. We really can't understand what people go through unless we have been there ourselves. However, I knew he was praying, probably not for himself, but for the rest of us if he didn't make it. I know I was praying which is the best thing we can do. The Guest Services person pushed that big button on the wall and the double doors opened. We walked into a short hallway and there it was on the wall: the schedule for the surgery rooms. Room 1: EICH Heart Transplant, Room 2: Organ Harvest. That is when it hit me. The donor was just next door or across the hall. It didn't matter which. What mattered was the donor was right there. My heart leaped when I saw EICH. This was really going to take place—the wait was about over.

We were taken to the pre-op room and a nurse came in, introduced herself and said she was giving Jack his 1st anti-rejection shot. Then we were told to say our words to him and she would take him in a few minutes. So I went first. I have never been good at this type of conversation. I took his hand; sedation was taking over as his eyes were quite droopy by now. I don't remember what I said to him but reflected on what a great life and love we had had so far and we still had much more to do before our earthly life together was over. I do remember distinctly what he said to me: "I love you. If I don't make it, promise me you will make sure my organs that can be are donated." It still brings tears to my eyes as I write this. We had barely mentioned the fact that he might not make it. We did make sure all our papers and things were in order should he die before getting a heart or during/after the surgery. But it was not part of our daily conversation. We were always upbeat and positive all would be okay, feeling the Lord was in charge, walking ahead and with us each step of the way. And yet, this last statement from Jack is typical of his character: generous, giving, putting others first. Then our sons, Jeff and John, stepped up to the bed as I stepped away and went to stand with Kim. Both had tears in their eyes. The boys, as we still call them, both hold their dad in high esteem and Jack adores them. I've always felt their tight bonds and strong work ethics were developed in our work truck during the months of mowing grass together. Jack started a lawncare business to supplement our income and give the boys jobs without doing the fast-food thing. This meant a lot of "truck time" with Dad while growing up, making the boys captive audiences.

As the boys leaned over the bed, Jack's voice was becoming slower and more deliberate. He said to the boys, "You two have turned out great and I don't know how." Kim and I looked at each other and chuckled. Where was I in the picture of raising the boys? Just then the nurse came and said, "It is time to go." She gave us directions as to where to wait, said someone would call us at various points in the surgery. I'm glad someone else was listening as I was focused on Jack being wheeled away. Surely our wonderful life together wasn't over. God had brought us this far, he would stick by us. The problem with that thought is that God didn't promise all would be hunky-dory. He promised He would be with us through everything. "... **And behold, I am with you always, even to the end of the world" (Matthew 28:20, ESV).** That includes the passing of those dearest to us. I knew that to be true having lived through the passing of my precious mother in 1997. So off he went and there I stood leaning on the Lord for whatever was to come. It was 10:30 P.M.

It was too late to go to the daytime cardiac waiting room that I knew well, the one with the friendly welcoming staff, the TVs, the free coffee and tea, the comfy chairs in the pleasant colors, pretty woodwork dividing the large room into cozy sections. Instead we headed to some other waiting room as the nurse had directed us. There was no one there, just the furniture. Jeff, Kim, John and I took our places on the chairs to wait out a long night. Within a few minutes, a maintenance man came to say we had to leave as this room was soon to be locked for the night. We asked where we should go and he suggested another waiting room on another floor. He graciously took us there. There was another family there awaiting word on their loved one that had been shot. We settled in on the other side of the room. These chairs didn't look nearly as comfortable as the ones in the day cardiac waiting room. They were all single chairs connected by shared wooden arms with no possibility of even curling up in a horizontal position. We each slowly took a seat, ready for a long wait through the night.

At 11:00 P.M., just as we were settled in our seats, Pastor Rob Shrader appeared at the door. Rob was our pastor in London, a six-hour distance away. We were all so glad to see him that I think we all said "Rob" in unison. Rob had become special to our family as he ministered to us during this time of difficulty. He had come unexpectantly to the CMC Hospital when Jack had his pacemaker/defibrillator inserted in 2005. I remember his tall body appearing at the door of the recovery unit at that time. It was the first time he had met Jeff and John as his ministry in London was just beginning. He had a black eye from some basketball game so it gave us a light moment of discussion. Jack was so glad to see him. Rob is the same age as our oldest, Jeff. While Rob was with us in 2005, one of the doctors came by and asked if he was our son. He could pass as our son as he has the same coloring as Jack. We were proud to say he was our pastor. It was so comforting to join hands with Jeff, John, Jack and Rob and have Rob pray over Jack at that time. So once again it was comforting and joyful to see him. After a few words of "we didn't know you were coming" and "how much we appreciate you coming all this way to be with us," we circled for prayer for Jack, the surgeons, nurses and other medical personnel in the room (who knew how many that was). It was one of the most peaceful times of my experience, as I know Jesus was right there with us. Afterwards, we settled in for the long night, each taking part in the "waiting chatter" of helpless loved ones in waiting rooms.

I had noticed the location of the telephone when we first came in the room. I knew I would jump at the sound of it for any word on Jack. It did ring at about 12:40 A.M. It seemed so loud; I jumped up immediately and ran to pick it up. There was a nurse on the other end to inform me that the surgery had begun at 12:30 A.M. She would call me with updates. They took him from us at 10:30 and two hours later it was just getting started. Time was moving slowly. As we talked, we all became drowsy. But there was not to be any sleeping for me. At times my thoughts rolled over to our donor's family. Were they up too, unable to sleep because of their grief? How sad they must be. Jeff, Kim and John dozed off, looking so uncomfortable. John and Jeff both walk around in over 6' frames, 6'6" and 6'5" to be specific. They looked crunched in those chairs, but seemed to be sleeping just fine. Rob and I continued to talk continuously. We have laughed since about our all-nighter because we can't remember the topics we covered, but they seemed so interesting at the time. How the Lord can provide what we need when we need it. At about 2:45, the phone rang again. I was so glad I wasn't asleep when it rang. The same nurse told me Jack's fresh heart had begun to beat on its own at 2:30 A.M. All was going well and she would call again when the surgery was over. Tears filled my eyes and I suddenly felt weak with joy and relief as I told the rest of the waiting group. I wanted so badly to call Emily but didn't because of the time. One cannot express enough praise and thanksgiving to the Lord at a time like this. All the waiting, the pleas to God, the good wishes of people all come together in one overwhelming moment. We all jumped up and down a bit and then settled back in our chairs. Rob prayed again. This one was for thanksgiving. The others went back to sleep but Rob and I talked on. The phone rang again. It was 4:30 A.M. Jack was off the heart and lung machine. The doctor would come to see us as soon as possible but he still had much work to do. So the long wait was basically over. Prayers had been answered as requested. God had watched over all involved. Sometimes the realness of God is more than we can explain. This wasn't the only time in my life I felt this, but it was the strongest. Can you recall some of those times in your life?

We waited on Dr. Reames to come, not knowing how long it would be. At 5:30 A.M., here he came through the door, still wearing his surgical garbs, whites and surgical hat. As soon as he gained eye contact with me, he threw both arms up in the air and declared, "I feel good about this one!" His joy was so apparent it made my own heart leap with joy as I ran to him. Big smile, friendly, hearty handshake and eyes that looked deep into mine. He said all went well and the fresh heart had started right up as soon as Jack's warm blood hit it. Was this the same doctor that had spoken to me pre-surgery, the one with his game face on? The one that had made my heart sink at the possibility of non-stop blood oozing from Jack's former scar tissue? It sure was. How grateful I was that he had his game face on and was focused on Jack's transplant surgery. How grateful I was now that God had given us Dr. Reames. He had been spending untold hours in medical school while I was raising children and supporting Jack's coaching career. Makes one wonder what people that will cross your path in the future in some spectacular God planned way are doing today to be ready for that day. Or what are we doing to prepare us for such an event. God's plan is so big for each of us. As humans, we cannot comprehend how it all fits together. Yet when we see a tiny piece of it in our own lives it is so amazing. As Pastor Farrell Lemings of Grace Covenant Church once said in a sermon, "God is seldom early, but never late." That had been so true for me. My impatience with God and his timing the two weeks before was a waste of my energy and an undisciplined act as God had the perfect heart for Jack in his timing. Any donor's heart other than the one Jack received would not have been perfect for him. We serve and are loved by an amazing God that has a different time clock than we humans operate on. How difficult it is to abide by that fact. Dr. Reames went on to tell us he had been looking for us and didn't know where we had been.

The cardiac waiting room was again open for another day but we did not think or know to move to it. He instructed us to move to the cardiac waiting room and we would be able to see him in the ICU in a few hours. Rob prayed a prayer of thanksgiving, hugged each of us and left for a hotel room to rest up before the long drive back. He said he would call before he left.

CHAPTER 8

Post-Surgery - Walking the Pathway in Faith and Joy

March 4, 2007: We all gathered our things, headed to the cardiac waiting room to set up "Eicher shop" for a few days. The two receptions were familiar to me as I had gotten to know them when Jack was hospitalized for the defibrillator implant and the transplant testing. They were excited that Jack had received his transplant. It is a blessing how people can quickly become close friends when they are so concerned with your needs.

At 10:00 A.M. only I was permitted to visit Jack in ICU. I knew what the picture would look like—Jack with tube coming out of his mouth, IVs still in, several machines with colored lines beeping and Jack out cold. I had seen that same scene on his other three heart/valve surgeries so the "room scene" did not shock me. However, there were a couple of things that amazed me and brought me to tears. His ears looked a different color than before surgery. They were pink and it seemed I could see the blood flowing through. The nurse said he was beginning to try to wake up and she was keeping him out longer, adding he was doing remarkable. Although he was unresponsive, the nurse said I could hold his hand. When I uncovered his right hand, I said to her, "They don't look like his hands." The color change was remarkable. I then remembered Dr. Gulati asking me if he was always this color in our interview. I said yes at the time, not realizing how off his color was. The color change had happened slowly over time and was not noticeable to me. It is like that when you are with someone every day. That drastic color change was the first indication of how life changing this transplant would be to us. I held his hand in mine, fluctuating between tears and feelings of uncontrollable joy. While I am a person that can jump up and down when good news is obvious, it just didn't seem appropriate at that moment in that room. So I contained my urge to jump up and down, feeling like I might explode from within. There he was. A man with a short lifespan just hours ago now with a "fresh" heart, donated by a person generous enough to give everything they could from their mortal life to a person they have never seen, known or will ever know. Well, maybe that statement will be corrected in heaven. We'll have to wait and see.

After my time was up, I thanked the nurse for taking care of my beloved Jack and headed back to my little corner of the cardio waiting room to settle in until the next visitation time @ 1:00 P.M. Soon after getting there, a man I had never met approached me and introduced himself as Pastor Paul Turbedsky from Grace Covenant Church. I was humbled that he had come to see me since we had never met. He spent time with me asking how Jack had done and how I was doing after staying awake all night. I don't know about you, but holding all-nighters is a thing of the past for me. I was on an emotional high but my body was tired from the inside out. Pastor Paul had hoped to also see Jack and pray over him but the ICU was closed to any visitors at that time. It was comforting to have him there. Before he left, he prayed for Jack's continued recovery and then prayed a prayer I had never heard before. He prayed that I would double the rest for the sleep I got. Those words stuck in my ears. I have heard and said so many prayers in my life as a Christian; many widely varied requests to the Lord from safe travel to saving the dying stated in different ways, different ways to say thank you to the Lord, and simple conversations with the Lord. But I had never heard this one—double the rest for the sleep one gets. It made me feel better and more rested already.

After a while of conversing and feeling as if I had a new Christian brother, he left. I passed the time with magazines and watching TV and watching the clock. Emily, Herb and Joseph had arrived from Nashville. Life felt even better and those hugs were oh, so good. A few minutes before 1:00, the receptionist called my name along with others to be escorted up to ICU. We all followed her like elementary children heading to the school cafeteria, saying little and exchanging polite smiles. I was expecting the same out of Jack as the 10:00 A.M. visit—out cold, tubes attached, eyes closed. The nurse had told me before that some patients were out for 24 hours to days, depending on "how they are doing." But alas, when I laid my eyes on him, he was in a slightly reclined position, eyes opened and tube gone from his mouth. He actually said "Hi" and started talking to me. I could not believe it! I so wish I had written down the words of our conversation that day. It was another one of my "wanting to jump up and down for joy" moments. I may have jumped a bit; I simply do not remember. I do remember the feeling of being in the midst of a miracle with the Lord standing right there with us. And I do remember the next conversation. The awesome nurse looked me straight in the eye and ordered me to go home and sleep for a while. Jack was doing great. I could call her directly and she would call me if necessary and I needed my rest for the time ahead. I agreed. Joseph, our young grandson, was also needing a nap, so Herb, Joseph and I headed to the house. My bed was calling my name LOUDLY by this time.

Just as I was crawling in, Rob called to check on Jack before he left, assuming he was still unconscious. When I told him, he was awake and talking; Rob could not believe it and wanted to see him. 4:00 P.M. was the next visiting time so he said he would go back to the hospital and wait. I hit the bed and fell asleep immediately while back at the hospital, Rob, Jeff, John and Emily awaited the 4:00 hour. They were all able to visit with him and once again he was wide awake and talking.

47

When I awoke a few hours later, I expected that groggy almost a headache feeling we experience when not getting enough sleep or sleep patterns are off. Sometimes it is better not to try to catch up on sleep as you feel worse when you get up. You probably know the feeling. And yet as I put my feet on the floor and stretched a bit, I felt perfectly fine as if I had had a full night's sleep! I called the nurse right away and she reported he was doing super. Then I remembered Pastor Paul's prayer for me—double the rest for the sleep I get. Answered prayer right there in my body. I would continue to be able to sleep well and feel energetic throughout Jack's recovery. I have adopted this prayer for others in similar situations and have shared my prayer with them. Isn't it a great Christian trait that we can take what others do for us, make it a part of us and pass it on to others? I believe that is how Jesus planned it and is pleased with us when we serve others as we have been served.

After the 4:00 visit, all three of our children, spouses and children came back to our house for dinner. Our children were all so joyful—unspeakable joy! Jeff was the one that described it as such. Not only had we all been blessed with Jack's transplant to give him a second life so to speak, but he was making a miraculous recovery. A transplant is different from a loved one surviving a death-threatening condition. That type of recovery, miraculous as it may be, is usually somewhat slow and brings an off and on joy over a period of time. Whereas, in a transplant the chance to survive is quick. A loved one is on a direct path to death and within hours the death causing organ is gone and a new healthy one is in its place. Your loved one is going to be with you here on earth for some time longer. The joy that comes from that realization is unspeakable. We had a very joyful dinner, discussing how amazing Jack was and any funny things he had said in ICU. He would not remember any of those funny things he said. After dinner, Emily and John went back to the hospital for the 8:30 P.M. visiting time. They came back smiling and reported he seemed totally normal. WOW!

We all got a great night's sleep that night. I called about 5:30 A.M. to check on Jack. A new nurse was on duty and she said he was doing great and to call before coming to the 10:00 A.M. visitation as he may be going to a room that day. His own room already? Really? That seemed like impossible news. I hung up the phone, tears of joy filled my eyes and said a prayer of thanks to our God that seemed to be sitting right there with me on the edge of my bed.

Emily and Herb needed to head back to Missouri so she was going to go with me to the 1:00 P.M. visit. When I called and checked again on him, I was told he was being moved and to wait in the cardiac waiting room to be called when they got him settled in his room. Amazingly by 1:30 he was in back on the cardiac floor in a private room along with Emily and me, where just two days ago the nurses were prepping him for the transplant surgery. The miracles and joy continued. Late in the afternoon, the transplant team came by to do their medical checks, congratulating him on how well he had done. I don't know about other transplant recipients, but heart transplant recipients are very emotional. Jack's emotions were beginning to show. One of the team members asked if he had any questions. With a shaky voice and with tears in his eyes, the only question he asked was, "Can this heart be donated again?" That's his question, I thought. All that is happening within his body and that is his question. I was greatly humbled as I don't think that would have been my first question upon seeing the transplant team for the first time. However, after I thought about it, that has always been the thought process for Jack, others first. After all, his last words to me before heading to surgery was to make sure his organs would be donated if he didn't make it. The answer to his question was no. His fresh heart had been through too much trauma, but his other organs could be. He was relieved to hear that. He apologized for the emotions but they reassured him, these emotions were perfectly normal. Later in the afternoon, he walked down the hall with a physical therapist. Simply amazing! To see someone walk down the hall with several tubes still attached filled my heart with more joy. Wasn't sure there was room left for more joy, but more came in. By the way, Jack had that big Eicher grin as he walked. It had to hurt him somewhere but at that moment, pain didn't matter.

"You have done many things for us, O Lord our God; there is no one like you! You have made many wonderful plans for us. I could never speak them all–their number is so great!" (Psalms 40:5, GNB).

March 6: Jack sat up in chair, walked again a bit farther. Although he couldn't tell it, blood tests were revealing that his kidneys were acting up a bit from the trauma and the medicine. If you recall, we had been told previous to surgery that Jack's kidneys were not fully functioning. But that could be expected in a patient that had taken medication for so many years. Doctors reassured us that his "kidney numbers" were temporary and would come back to his normal, which still wasn't normal, in time. I couldn't help remembering Susan's word of some patients need a kidney transplant after a heart transplant. I started to imagine being on that waiting list before long. Then I thought, what has happened to my faith? I had been praising God with prayers of thanksgiving on how well everything had gone. Not only had God taken us to this amazing point but had walked right next to us and even prepared a pathway before us. Now one negative issue and the fear factor was setting in. Why does this happen to us? I believe it is because we are human and the devil loves to sneak into our being and cause us to fear something, anything, losing focus on our Lord. I heard many times that there are 365 "fear nots" in the Bible. I don't have people to credit the quote to because I don't remember who they were. But I do remember them saying that was one "fear not" for every day of the year. With these thoughts, I took a deep breath and gave that back to the Lord. And you know what, it is thirteen years plus since those kidney numbers were way out of whack and his numbers today are better than before surgery. Jack does all he can to take care of those half-functioning kidneys, lots of water, little salt, etc. That doesn't mean that we will can forget that a kidney transplant might be in our future, but until then the Lord is holding on to that one for us. More important, at the moment the 2D Echo test was being performed. The 2D Echo is a type of ultrasound that allows a view into the heart and measures pressures. Jack's fresh heart looked good! The blessings continued. **"Don't be afraid, only believe" (Mark 5:36, GNB).**

Although Jack wasn't supposed to have visitors, due to his much-compromised immune system, four of our friends from our Sunday School Class at Grace somehow slipped in. I was so glad to see them that I jumped up and hugged all four of them. The nurse saw them go in the room and said they could only stay a few minutes and had to stand as far away from Jack as possible. It was so touching that they would take time to come and see us. After all, our friendships were fairly new. We had only been at the church for three and a half months. But during that time, our Sunday school class had embraced us and prayed every Sunday in class for us. I remember our first day in that class. Our son, Jeff, and his family attended Grace Covenant. When we were in town we would go with them. I just loved the spirit of the worship service there. Everything was so uplifting. When we started our heart wait, we went there. Jack and I have always been a part of a Sunday school class since we were married. I even taught a few years at two of our churches. It seemed that being in a class our Christian faith grew. Hearing lessons, sharing with Christian friends and discovering spiritual truths helped both of us in our Christian walk. We looked at the class offerings at Grace, selected one that sounded appropriate for us and just went. Of course, we were asked to introduce ourselves. Not too many newcomers appear with a portable pump around their waist resembling a fanny pack and looking a bit "green." As Jack told his story and our reason for being in that place at that time, our names were put on the prayer list right away and a prayer was said. We were prayed for each week thereafter. I felt so close to each of the people, not even knowing their names yet. Pam, the teacher, had a lesson each week that seemed to be just what I needed that week. It is comforting to know the Lord's plan includes giving a person the words they need just at the right time. We never missed a Sunday during our wait. Jack says that Jeff brought us to Grace, but God lead us to Pam's class. During that time, the class had social events allowing us to make some very special friends that will always have a special place in our hearts. The class has since disbanded due to changes in church scheduling, but we are now partners at Grace and still have friendships with many in that class.

An email to update our friends, school faculty and family:

From: Jack & Carol Eicher
Sent: Wednesday, March 07, 2007 8:41 A.M.
To: Subject: Jack and his new heart are doing great!

Hi to all,
Please excuse this general type e-mail. I'm writing from home-if you're in my home email you are probably getting this.

As most of you know (I apologize to those of you who don't-it has been a whirlwind), Jack received a new heart Sun AM-the heart started beating at 2:30 AM! He is doing super, exceeding all expectations of the Drs. We appreciate and can feel the strength of the many prayers you have said, thought and shared with us. I ask that you now request from our gracious Father above that the medicine for anti-rejections will not need to be very strong, that his body will accept the heart of this most generous person without much medicine. The medicine is very hard on the kidneys.

Our path to where we are today has been made so easy by the Lord. We have faith it will continue to be so through prayers and our continued faith. We will be forever grateful to the donor and their family. Our hope is that they will decide to meet us in due time. How can we ever say thank you???????

If you are not already an organ donor, please let Jack be your inspiration to sign up. The joy this has brought us as a family is unspeakable.

Take care and love to all,
Carol

Do you have a friend or friends that could be classified as a soulmate? Those people you felt instantly connected to upon first meeting? You know the one(s) you don't see or talk with for long periods of time but when you connect with them by phone or face to face, it is as if there was no gap in your time together. God doesn't give many true friends to us in life. They are one of God's greatest blessings to us. Who are yours? Those few people that would do anything for you and you for them, that you feel spiritually connected to and have times of longing to be with them. Take time to thank God for the people and make a connection with them soon. One of such friends is Marna Bundy of London, Kentucky. We first met at her house shortly after Jack was hired to be the head football coach at Laurel County. Her husband, Clemons, was the AD for the Laurel County School District and had been instrumental in hiring Jack. He had also been instrumental in Jack deciding to take the job at Laurel County High School and move our family to the southeastern part of Kentucky. The down-to-earth approach Clemons displayed and his concern for the students in Laurel County was one factor that sold Jack, along with the fact that we felt the Lord was drawing us to Laurel County. Little did we know the great love affair we would have with the area and the people we would meet.

Back to Marna: She and I connected immediately upon being introduced at her home in the spring of 1988. They had invited us to come for dinner as we were camping in the area over spring break while Jack was working in the weight room and preparing to start a successful football program. Have I mentioned yet that Jack is the winningest coach in Laurel County? Anyway, we had an enjoyable time with them, as did our children and theirs, feeling as if they had been part of our lives long before their generous hospitality. She and I were connected from then on. Some people even claim we look alike and have been mistaken as the other person. For a couple days after Jack's transplant, she and I had been playing that frustrating game of phone tag. When we finally got to talk to each other, it was uplifting for me to hear her voice. After asking how Jack and I were doing, she said, "I owe you and Jack an apology." I responded with, "What on earth for?" She said, "I knew Jack's surgery would go through the night, so I promised myself that I would pray as needed. I'm sorry to say that I fell asleep at 2:30 A.M." Chills instantly went through my body as tears filled my eyes as the work of the Lord stuck me with such strength I was almost unable to answer. "Oh, Marna," I said, "Jack's heart started beating on its own at exactly 2:30 A.M." She simply gasped then sighed; you know the kind of sigh when there are no words, when you know that the Lord is so very active in your life when you are not aware of the miracle of which you are a part. We cannot measure or even comprehend His overwhelming love for us. Neither can we understand in our humanness how He is at work in the details our lives. Marna and I simply rejoiced and had a God moment together, realizing the awesome blessing of the Lord in our lives, the miracles of prayer and our love for each other. Many Christians have stories of "praying across the miles." This is one of mine and the most touching. I have shared this God moment with many people and it always gives the listener chills. The unveiling or revealing of miracles among Christians is always a joy and a reinforcement of the blessings of the Christian life. Take time to give some thought to your life. When have you had miracles unveiled? They can be in your life or when hearing of the miracles in other lives. I love how Christians often gasp when hearing these. You can hear it especially if sharing is done in a group or a classroom-type setting. It seems as if we can't believe it happened. But it isn't disbelief. It is another amazing moment in our Christian life of God revealing his mighty power and plan to His children. And we are amazed! How great Thou art!

March 8: This was a day of medical happening for Jack. The joyful and liberating happening was the removal of the chest tubes that assisted in the draining of the fluid that comes from the chest after any intrusion into the chest cavity. What a relief that was! Another happening had to do with drainage of his leg. The heart and lung machine tubes had been run thru his leg/groin area for medical reasons that now escape me. On this day, his leg stopped draining. The doctors were surprised. I'm not sure if that was a good thing as you will see later, but it seemed good to me at the time. Jack had begun walking the hospital halls as much as possible with the help of the physical therapist or a nurse. Of course, we were restricted to the hall with the telemeters so his heart could be monitored with every step. With the chest tubes out and one less piece of equipment to roll along (he was still toting IVs) this next walk was going to be a great one. After a short "freedom" walk that day and returning to his room, he felt excruciating pain in the back of his head and neck. His face grimaced and his hand rushed to grasp his neck when the pain hit. It was such a shock to both of us. Scared me to the bone as I thought something had seriously gone wrong. Up to this point, all the pain had been manageable through the use of those miracle drugs and Jack's plain old toughness. I called a nurse right away. Blood pressure was taken and it had shot up a bunch. After some rest and time, the pain subsided. Doctors were unable to give us a cause for this, perhaps the way his head was turned during surgery. This headache, after exercise, would be a lingering after effect of the transplant for many months, even showing up occasionally years later. However, it did not come after every exercise session. Later, it would usually come when we were in the car and he was driving and be specific to his neck. The true cause was never determined. A blot clot also formed in his arm, which we were told was nothing serious, but a result of the pic line. His creatinine was also still rising. That is a sign the kidneys are not happy. We had been warned that kidney problems could follow as the antirejection meds are so hard for the kidneys to process and Jack already had kidney damage from all the years of medication. The doctors were very comforting and told us all of these things were to be expected and Jack was still doing awesome. I said many prayers that day—that things would calm down and tomorrow would be a better day. However, my most often stated prayer was "Thank you that Jack is still with me." Despite the trials that were there, my heart was still overjoyed to the point of often being giddy. Of course, I wasn't the one experiencing the pain and test results. I even shared with Jack that at least he was still on earth to feel the pain. Probably not much comfort to him. But, it did make me feel better.

The next day, March 9, was not quite as tumultuous. Ultrasounds were done to check the small blood clot in his arm. The catheter was taken out which was a great relief for him. We just kept getting closer to not being attached to anything. He could take two walks with the painful headache appearing after the second one. A stomachache accompanied it. Once again we were told that that would probably stop with time—not to worry. Even with the medical happening, each day was uplifting and a day of great thanksgiving. I was overwhelmed with gratefulness that Jack had been given this great gift of a heart was still alive. We would talk about things we wanted to do when he was healed. Had he not been given this gift, we would have been discussing funeral arrangements. One thing he promised if all turned out okay was to take all our adult children and grandchildren to Disney World. Now that was something to look forward to.

March 11: Sunday, we were told that we could go home, our NC home, the next day if there was no rejection on the biopsy which would be done on Monday. Go home? Was I ready for that? It had only been six days. That was shorter than his first heart surgery in Texas. I was excited to hear that great news and of course, Jack was more than ready. But me? This was time to pray for peace and strength to enter unchartered territory. I did and waited for peace to come which it did. We were also told that day that the kidneys were beginning to come back. The numbers had stopped heading in the wrong direction and were now heading in the right direction. More prayers answered as requested. I left the hospital that night, excited that the next time I left, I would have my precious Jack with me. I slept great that night.

I was at the hospital early that day to be there while Jack faced one of what would be many biopsies. The nurses and doctors had hoped to get him in early so the results of the biopsy would be available and we could head home. Checking for rejection in heart tissue is not an immediate result test. It takes some time to work the medical magic that would become our reassuring safety net for months to come. Medical timing does not always go as planned. And today was one of those days. And that was alright. The rooms that are used for the biopsies are also the rooms used for heart caths. There were some patients that needed medical attention before Jack. They were emergency-type situations. So we patiently waited. I continued my reading of endless magazines. Helped to pass the time. I have always felt for those that needed to be put ahead of me, Jack or my children in any medical situation. Emergencies are just that—emergencies. Jack was not an emergency, at least not on this day.

Finally, Jack's turn came late in the day and the biopsy was complete. However, not in time for us to hear the results before heading to our North Carolina home. Jack was feeling very tired after the long wait. The results came back with 0 rejection! A result all heart transplant recipients hope for. We once again looked forward to the next tomorrow to go home. Another bit of good news was the bloodwork showed his kidneys were functioning as pre-transplant. This was just as exciting as the 0 rejection.

March 13: I woke up early, excited to know I would be bringing Jack home on this very day. When I got to the hospital, Jack was mentally ready to just walk out. Of course, we had to see a transplant doctor or nurse, be trained in the life time dispensing of medicine, complete all the necessary paperwork and wait for Guest Services to come with a wheelchair. Jack always detested the wheelchair ride. After one of his previous heart surgeries, he tired of waiting, refused the wheelchair and we walked straight out. Typical of Jack's personality. But on this day we waited for the wheelchair. Our hearts were so full of thankfulness at this point it really didn't matter and after all, we had promised to follow all of the rules. Following the rules was the best guarantee for a long second life for Jack.

To the car I walked while Jack headed out in a wheelchair. I was instructed to get the car and drive to the front of the hospital and pick up Jack. As I started to walk away, I was filled with so much unexpected emotion. My chest felt full of joy, I wanted to break out skipping rather than walking. But where were those tears coming from? It was a moment like none before. My trip to the car was one I will never forget. Then driving to the front of the hospital, I thought of the drop off ten days earlier. I was unable to speak the words "heart transplant" to the attendant that had been watching and waiting for our arrival. An arrival of a man heading toward death and a wife almost too nervous to drive yet knowing Jesus had it all under control. Ten days of difference— from delivering a slowly dying heart to picking up a young fresh heart strongly beating. The realization of God's miracles in our lives is sometimes overwhelming.

I managed to drive where I was supposed to be and there he was, sitting in that wheelchair with that big Eicher grin I was so glad to see. He gingerly stepped into the car, put on his seatbelt and we were off to our NC home, about 20 minutes away. He looked over at me and said, "We did it." Yes, we did it! Walked a remarkable journey knowing we were living God's plan for our lives. On the way home, Jack expressed his thankfulness to be alive and in this world. That, of course, was a ditto for me.

Walking into our house was absolutely wonderful. The morning hospital activities and the ride home had worn Jack out. He headed straight to the couch and I set up all we had to keep track of—meds, blood test schedules, diabetes testing.

Nurse Katie called shortly after we were home to see how we were doing. It was so reassuring to hear her voice and I relayed to her that Jack had said he was so glad to be here. She said here, where? When I said alive on this earth, she responded, "We didn't have any doubts about that!" Made me feel great to know they thought success was a sure thing. There was a great feeling of peace to be safely at home with Jack's doctors and nurses just a phone call and a few miles away. But challenges would come upon us in the future.

"Give thanks to the Lord..." (Psalms 105:1, GNB).
"...Remember the miracles that God performed..."
(Psalms 105:6, GNB).

Email on March 13th, 2007

Hello to all,
Once again we have 0 rejection from the biopsy! It was taken on Monday. We are dealing with a few minor items that are typical of post transplant patients, nothing that can't be worked out or through. We are really excited! God continues to bless us, not only through this but with great and caring friends. Jack sends his most sincere thanks to all of you for your kind words, thoughts, cards and most of all your prayers!

Hello to every dedicated educator at SLHS. 1st one of you that reads this, please send out to the rest. I'm going to check my school email to see who wins! GO!

Love to all,
Carol

CHAPTER 9

On the Pathway of Recovery to Normal

March 14: While in the hospital, Jack had covered many hallways while walking as instructed. He was so ready to get well and knew walking was a huge key to make that happen. Of course, when we were home, we wanted to continue and increase the walking. As we walked the sidewalks of our street, his ankles began to swell. Now that was a scary event to us since swelling of the ankles is a sign of heart failure and the signs of rejection of the new heart were the same. He had lived with swollen ankles off and on for many years. I called the transplant nurse. She said that was okay and normal. We both gave a sigh of relief. She explained that before surgery, his heart was unable to rid his body of fluid so he had a lot. It could take up to A YEAR for the new heart to rid his body of all the accumulated fluid. Now that seemed amazing to me. What a lengthy miracle of the human body. We found this to be true, even down to Jack's fingers. He had to quit wearing his wedding band after a while as it was too big for his slimmer left ring finger.

March 15: On this day, we began our many trips to Carolina Medical Center for routine blood tests which checked Jack's levels of Prograf and kidney function among many other medical conditions which I don't pretend to understand. Over time, the trips sort of had a homecoming feel as we were greeted warmly by Marcia, the person drawing Jack's blood. She was always friendly and so glad Jack was doing well. While Jack's blood tests are now much fewer and farther apart, we still head to CMC forgoing a shorter drive to another lab. It just feels right to go there.

March 16: One of the strangest things to me about Jack's recovery was the open hole in his abdomen where a drainage tube once was during the hospital stay. It was normal for liquid to ooze out. Sort of like watered-down blood. On this day, he had drainage from that hole for most of the day. We patched it and carried on knowing someday it would end.

We were ready for some new scenery during our walking time so we headed to our church, Grace Covenant. It is a large church that has a great hallway that circles the entire building. Jack even did a few steps to the second floor. We took off walking and then it happened. The extreme headache and sick to stomach feeling hit him, causing him to double over. It would be at the base of his skull, usually the right side with almost unbearable pain. This had happened while in the hospital but not since we had been home. No one knew the source of this. Guesses included position of his head during surgery or muscle cramps. It came and went throughout his recovery. On occasion, it will still show up only not with the same severity.

March 17: Jack was up to 5000 steps of walking by this date. Amazing! Walked 5000 steps in one day, thirteen days after surgery. The strange draining events would start again and then stop. We would think they were over and then suddenly there would be a wet spot on his shirt. I would wonder, hasn't this hole healed yet? I guess the body takes care of itself after such trauma. We are awesomely made! **"I praise you, for I am fearfully and** wonderfully made. Wonderful are your works; my soul knows it very well" (Psalms 139:14, ESV).

March 19: Jack scored another 0 rejection on a biopsy. That was the best news we could hear but something was looming, swelling in the groin. The swelling began to move slowly down his right leg. The doctors ordered an ultrasound and continued to keep an eye on it. He and his heart were doing just fine.

March 21: Jack's mood was down a bit as the swelling remained in his right leg. Even with the swelling, he managed to fertilize the yard. His words were, "If I can walk, I can do this." I have learned over the years not to nag or fight the Eicher-man attitude as I get nowhere. Amazingly, he felt better and more upbeat in the evening.

March 23: In the morning, I realized I had been giving Jack 500 mg of Cellcept twice a day rather than 1000 mg twice a day since Monday. Five days of one-half of the anti-rejection meds. How sick I felt! Would I be responsible for heart rejection? We had four more days until another biopsy. Only time would tell. I will say I did some intense praying with a specific request for the next three days. Jack was not nearly as concerned with my mistake as I was. I suppose he was doing some specific praying also.

March 26: Jack was up to walking almost two miles each day now and feeling great, except for that nagging swollen groin.

March 27: Biopsy Day! I admitted to the nurse my medicine mistake. She reassured me it would be okay but I was still very concerned. Prayers were answered as the news was almost all good. A big fat 0 on rejecting and Jack's kidney function was improving. However, surgery was scheduled for the next day to correct whatever was making the right leg swell.

March 28: Surgery was done to correct lymph glands in Jack's right groin by Dr. Reames. I thought it was comforting to have the same doctor that performed the heart transplant doing this surgery. I knew we were in great hands. The surgery took longer than I thought it would during which I caught myself thinking something had gone wrong. But all went well. When I went to the recovery room, there was Nurse Susan, sitting with Jack to make sure he and his fresh heart were doing just fine. We were so glad to see Susan as she had been off on maternity leave.

Our son, John, was living in our house while his was on the market. It was another miracle of comfort for me to have him in the house. He was with me all that day. Jack came home the next day. Another drainage tube attached to him, but feeling good. He soon made a full recovery from the groin surgery.

April 1, 2007: Our great friends from London, Wayne and Lynne Keen, came to visit Jack. It was such a joy to see them. Wayne coached with Jack at Laurel County and South Laurel. He and Lynn were a big part of the welcoming committee on the day we moved to London. They were amazed at how great he looked and how well he felt.

Apr. 2: A biopsy was done with a 0 rejection. I was loving these 0s. Because of this great score, Jack's Prednisone was lowered. A big step on the pathway to normal. Seeing members of the transplant team and those working in the biopsy waiting room each time was comforting. They became family to us.

April 15: We had hit six-week mark out from transplant surgery! What a miracle!

Apr. 17, 2007: Another 0 biopsy! Feeling great! Ankles still swollen. Kidneys were improving! We were told by one of the doctors we could go back to London. What? Already? This was hard to believe. I was not expecting this miracle. I wasn't sure I was even ready for it. We went back to our house and started packing.

April 18: We left Moss Creek in the morning with mixed emotions. I looked back at the house as I drove out of our very short driveway, feeling so thankful for all that had taken place. But also with a a deep in the gut fear of heading into the unknown. Were we ready for this? Was I ready for this? What if there was an emergency? I felt so secure being close to the hospital with the team of doctors and nurses which had become my safety net. But I bravely put my foot on the gas pedal and headed for "home." Thinking the trip of six and a half hours might be a bit much for Jack, we stayed in Gatlinburg for two nights. Gatlinburg is our favorite place to visit. It felt wonderful to be there again, filled with gratitude that Jack was alive. That stay would begin many trips back and forth in years to come.

April 20: We arrived in London, pulled onto our street, pushed the button in the car to raise the garage door, and pulled into our garage. We both filled up with tears as I turned the engine off. We were back home! Miracle! Neighbors and friends had taken great care of our house, inside and out, while we were gone for those eighteen weeks. We so appreciated that. As I walked into the house and into the family room, I broke out in laughter. I was not expecting what I saw. My small Christmas tree full of angels was still up right where I had left it after decorating before we left for our adventure full of miracles. None of those generous people watching our house had taken it down. So, there they were, guarding our house. Angels I had bought in special places, angels from friends as gifts, angels from family members. All there as symbols to guard our family home in the sweet town of London, Kentucky.

April 21: The very next day Jack mowed grass for a couple of his customers!!!!! I tried not to worry about this as he had been given permission from the heart doctors to do so. But he had to wear a mask and long sleeves with lots of sunscreen lathered on. But our friends in our beloved London had no idea of those rules. A few people called me to ask if I knew he was mowing. I would say yes. Then ask, "Does he have on a mask and long sleeves?" If they said yes, I would say he could do that. They would be amazed and who wouldn't be? It had only been six weeks since his surgery. What an amazing recovery path he was following. They also did not know had badly he wanted to get back to his normal life. His attitude through all of it was one of feeling so blessed by God's goodness and healing hand. When friends would say they were so sorry he or we were having a rough time, he would reply, "Oh, I am so blessed to be where I am." The Lord has blessed us. Although we have not been through other illnesses where death is a sure thing unless there is a cure, I would think those that have would feel the same, blessed beyond belief. Heart transplant is a cure for the recipient. Sure, there are heightened risks with a suppressed immune system and the possibility of rejection is always there. But to be able to continue living gives one such overwhelming feelings of thankfulness, joy, love for the donor and praise to God, the Greatest Healer of all.

"And he healed many who were sick with various diseases..." (Mark 1:34, ESV).
"And he went throughout all of Galilee, teaching in their synagogues and proclaiming the gospel of the kingdom and healing every disease and every affliction among the people" (Matthew. 4:23 ESV).

April 23: This was the day I went back to work, teaching at my beloved South Laurel High School. State testing was going on and I had not been there for the yearly required training so I was assigned to work with the seniors as they were exempt from the testing. Made for a pretty easy week. This might be a good place to mention the miracle of the sick days. Did you know God is a mathematician? In Kentucky at that time, sick days could build up over the years. I have been blessed with great health and rarely missed a teaching day due to illness. It was the same with my children. Therefore, I had a bunch of sick days saved up. When I finished that school year, after missing all that time while in North Carolina and making trips back for biopsies, I still had two sick days left. Two DAYS! I lost not one penny of pay. Now that is some remarkable math and timing on God's miracle working schedule. Just love the way he works for our good.

Apr. 27: Jesse and Jackson had a birthday party at a public park not far from their home. Those two boys were never content to stay in one place and would take off from a standing position like track stars at any moment. Jesse was the one that day that decided he would run as fast as possible to some unknown destination. To everyone else's surprise, Jack took off running after him. He had not been able to run for years! Jeff looked at me with eyes wide open and said, "Is he supposed to be running?" And he took off. They both caught up with Jesse and brought him back. Jack was smiling that giant grin of his as he could run again. Wasn't even winded. We all were so excited at this unbelievable positive change in health. God felt so close that day. Do you ever feel just totally wrapped up in his goodness? It was one of those days.
Emily and Herb had come for the weekend to see Jack and celebrate the birthdays. It was so good to have them there as they had not seen Jack since the day after his surgery. There is nothing better in life than to have your family all together.

Yes, another email.

From: Jack & Carol Eicher
Sent: Wednesday, May 02, 2007 9:17 P.M.
Subject: Jack scores another 0!!!!

Hi to all,
Jack scored another 0 on his biopsy! The pressures were also measured inside his heart. They are perfect! The drain tube in his groin lymph glands was taken out. We were waiting to see if the drainage stops before going back to London. Remarkably, it has stopped already! Jack is fearful

it may start again but I'm feeling another miracle in action. He had 600 cc of fluid drain the day before the surgeon removed the tube. For that to heal and stop that quickly is amazing. We are planning to return to London over the weekend.

Take care,
Carol

We continued the trek between London and Charlotte on a regular basis for heart biopsies and doctor checks. While it was rather demanding, I always found beauty in the drive. I always took papers to grade with me but often never touched them while in the car. I felt as if I had two homes. You know when you are gone on a trip and you return home and you think, oh, my bed feels so good? I felt like that in both places.

May 15: As we were driving back from the latest biopsy, we got a call from the nurse that the biopsy score was 1, meaning slight rejection. We were told it was okay and normal. I was not happy, though. I only wanted 0s. Those 0s always gave me a feeling of peace that all was well. The 1 gave me just a tinge of worry. Would it get worse and we would not know it? Those were the times when I wanted Charlotte to be home. To be close to that talented heart team.

May 26: I participated at graduation at SLHS, always a special day to send those students out into the world. That afternoon, Jack and I hiked at Cumberland Falls State Park. Awesome place! We always loved hiking there but this day was special as it was our first time there since the surgery.

May 29: Another biopsy, another email

From: Jack & Carol Eicher
Sent: Wednesday, May 30, 2007 7:54 P.M.

Subject: Jack gets another great score!

Hi to all,

Jack scored another 1, which is great according to the transplant staff. Due to Jack's competitive nature, he would like a zero. However, they have told us a 1 is great, so we are very thankful. Medicine has been lowered once again. We will now move to once a month biopsies (YEAH) which continue for at least a year. The next one is June 26th so we have some breathing room from a fixed traveling schedule.

After the PA spoke with Jack yesterday, she looked at the nurse there and said "Can't we just give him an A and let him be on his way?" He is the 1st heart transplant patient she can remember that had to be told to slow down. Isn't that so much Jack Eicher?????? He was given permission to start riding his bicycle again. I guess I better get mine cleaned off too!

I can see the Lord beginning to use Jack to serve others as they face the prospect of a heart transplant. He spoke to his first patient yesterday before we left the hospital. Of course, he did great. Hopefully, we will have other opportunities to help others along the way.

For those of you wondering how life is, we are pretty much back to normal. Jack is mowing and running his lawn business and I'm back to the school routine. It is amazing how great he feels and how much energy he has. I think of our donor almost everyday with thoughts of thanksgiving and wonder about the family and how they are doing. They will forever be a part of our family.

Take care and love to all,
Carol

June 2007

June 3: We went to Cincinnati and Northern Kentucky where we started on our bicycle riding adventures. We rode 18 miles on The Little Miami Rail Trail out of Loveland, Ohio. We had ridden Rail Trails in many places across the country but had been on a hiatus since Jack needed a heart transplant. Both of us had wondered if we could ever ride together again. To be back on a trail felt so good! I was so excited as we were starting, that I yelled out to another couple I did not know, "You are witnessing a miracle. He just had a heart transplant in March." They both smiled and yelled some positive words back I do not recall. I was filled with such abundant joy as we pedaled along. We were blessed that weekend to see my dad, my sister Cheri and brother Grady.

June 8: We drove to Missouri to see Emily, Herb and Joseph for a few days. Another bike ride found us doing nine miles with Emily in Cape Girardeau. I do believe these bike rides helped in Jack's recovery. They sure boosted my mental wellbeing.

June 25: Jack had a biopsy scheduled on the 26th so we headed to Charlotte early and visited Old Salem on this day. I just loved being able to travel and see new places. Every day I would thank God over and over that Jack was still with me. We headed there to bike on the American Tobacco Rail Trail. We rode fifteen miles that day. And I was so happy!

June 27 Email
From: Jack & Carol Eicher
Subject: Jack gets another great big 0!

Hi to all,
We are thrilled to report that Jack's heart biopsy on Tuesday came up with a 0! That means NO rejection of the heart at all. I'm not sure who was the most excited-Jack, me or the transplant nurse that reported it to him. The transplant staff is thrilled with his progress and just laughs with joy when he tells them his activity level, including his bike rides of 17 & 18 miles on rail trails. We rode the American Tobacco Trail (17 miles) on Monday near Chapel Hill. It was beautiful and a special place to feel close to God and say THANK YOU to Him several times over. The blessings keep coming!

We continue to travel between Charlotte and London, keeping people confused as to our where abouts. To those of you in our wonderful church family in London, if we are in London, we are with you on Sunday. We appreciate you missing us in church and wondering if all is well. Rob S. will be one of the 1st to know if problems arise. We are certainly blessed to have been given Rob as our pastor at 1st Christian.

Also Bill and Nancy Huber are grandparents! 3 month old Maggie is the daughter of Janine and her husband. She will send pics if you beg her to. If you want her email, let me know and I will send it to you. Their 2nd daughter, Kari, is a dentist in

Charlotte and is expecting. The Hubers plan to move to this area in the future. Smaller world!

Love and blessing to all,
Carol

June 29: We once again went to Gatlinburg. This time we rode the Gatlinburg Trail on our bikes, a total of eight miles.

June 30: On the way back to London, we hiked a part of the Cumberland Gap Trail. Jack was feeling so great!

July 8, 2007: We biked the Crockett Trail in Somerset. It was not even fully opened yet.

July 11: Jack and I rode The Tour de Kentucky, an organized fundraiser bike ride for the Gill Heart Institute at UK. Jack had been a part of their program before his transplant. Jack rode 30 miles; I was only good for 24. The man was physically recovered as far as I could see.

July 15: Drove to the Smoky Mountains National Park. There is just something about that place that draws us back. It seems God is there and the time spent there is such a spiritual renewal. Some folks have that feeling about the beach, but the mountains have always given us that feeling of peace. The Smokies draw us back on a regular basis. When we moved to London, one of the things that excited us was that we would be two and a half hours closer to The Great Smoky Mountains National Park and the unique city of Gatlinburg, TN. We took full advantage of that closeness and went as often as we could. Strange how things come around. Our children now migrate there just as we did. We stayed that night at the Tree Tops Resort which is just on the National Park boundary. A person can walk right into the park at the end of the Roaring Fork Motor Nature Trail which must be the most beautiful road in the Park. Traffic is one way so one feels safe walking on the somewhat narrow road. We walked two miles in the park and two miles back out that day. One detail I have yet to mention is the fact that it is an up the mountainside walk. For Jack to be able to do that (he did it better than me) was a miracle for the watching. To walk with him uphill and see, touch and breathe in God's beauty surrounding us was truly a special God-given time.

July 16: Beat the streets of Gatlinburg.
Hiked five miles on a nature trail.
Hiked four miles on Schoolhouse Gap Trail.

July 17: Chimney's Area in the Smoky Mountains National Park for a picnic.

July 18: Hiked with Mark and Julie. Remember our friends that had the study group in their home and prayed for Jack? That's them. We went six miles on the Little River Trail and Cucumber Trail in the Smokies.

July 19: Hiked 2.5 miles at the Cradle of Forestry & Blue Ridge Parkway.

July 20, 2007: Hiked three miles.

July 21: Hiked three miles. It was great to do all this hiking. Jack was feeling great!

July 23: We were back in our house in Concord for another biopsy.

Email update
From: Jack & Carol Eicher
Sent: Sun 7/29/2007 10:03 P.M.
Subject: Jack has another great biopsy!

Hello to all,

We were in Charlotte this past Monday for the monthly check and biopsy. Jack scored a 1 which the transplant team says is a great score. We feel a twinge of disappointment when it is not a 0, but at least we know the immune system is back up and working. Medicine was reduced again so it won't be too long until he is off the Prednisone completely. He feels great and we are back to normal. He has the deck floor torn up and is putting on a new one, I'm getting ready to start another school year. We rode our bikes 24 miles in the Tour de Kentucky a couple weeks ago. Jack rode 30 miles. I knew I would not be able to keep up with him and his 30 something heart! It was only a matter of time.

This will be my last biopsy report on a regular basis unless a problem arises. Since we have been blessed to return to a normal life and school will start soon, I don't feel they are necessary. We do want to thank each of you for your prayers and all the unlimited kindnesses you have extended to us and our family. This has been and continues to be a deeply spiritual experience. It is difficult to explain how comforting our relationship with the Lord has been to us and how much our family of friends have meant to us. My college roommate wrote to me about the many friends we must have because of the number of emails we send. How right she is and those are just the ones we have the address for! (I'm splitting this email as the last one I sent said I had too many recipients.) One of our greatest long term blessings has been the wonderful people we have met along the way and come to call friends in different places we have lived. We appreciate each of you.

Many people ask about our donor. We have written to our donor's family and think of them often. We have not yet heard from them and might not ever hear from them. We realize they are still grieving over their deep loss and may not be ready to contact us. Remember, there are 7 or more families who are still rejoicing as our donor gave all his/her organs. What wonderful gifts to leave behind. We will be forever grateful to the donor and the family.

Keep in touch. Blessings and good health to you and your families.

Take care and love to all,
Carol & Jack

August 12: Jack and I were asked one time to give a speech about our transplant experience. Well, it wasn't truly a speech. It was the sermon or message on August 12, 2007, at our church in London. It was more a time of sharing the goodness of God as we had experienced it in our journey of the heart transplant. Our pastor gave us the audio CD of it but I never listened to it until writing this book years later. While many of the things we shared are already a part of this book, it was so good to listen and hear the thankfulness in our voices for the miracles we had witnessed and experienced. It was also good to remember what the people of that church meant to us. That church was another step along our pathway, a piece of the jigsaw so to say. On that day, Jack spoke first. We were both a bit nervous, he more so than me. He shared the "Behold, I come quickly" story to lighten things up a bit. Then he showed and explained the quilt from KODA, Kentucky Organ Donors Affiliate. This is a quilt that honors the donors of organs across Kentucky. Each family of a donor makes a block to honor their family member. Someone then sews the blocks together and makes a quilt. There of course are many quilts. We were fortunate to have one to share with our congregation that day. They are certainly a moving and beautiful tribute to those who have given organs to people that they have never met. The tradition of the donor quilts is also done in North Carolina with a ceremony when the families bring their blocks to share. Jack then gave our children and their families credit for their immeasurable help in our journey and recovery. What a blessing it is when a person has people in his family that give a reason to live. Our children and grandchildren were those people to Jack. Although we had three grandchildren at the time, I knew in my heart, there would be more—more precious little people to love and watch grow with great happiness. One of my prayer requests for Jack to receive a heart and fully recover was to experience the joy he would have of knowing them and his lifetime effect on each of their lives. God has certainly answered that prayer. He shared what God has done for us in our lives. And the multitude of prayers answered and miracles that happened.

Then he shared his favorite Bible verses. Jack has always been what I refer to as a "quiet Christian." Those "quiet Christians" are deeply rooted in God's Word, living out God's commandments and promises daily. The verses he shared have shaped his adult life. The first one was I Cor. 10:13: God will not allow you to be tempted beyond your ability to endure. He shared his experience with that verse. "When you have the Lord walking with you it is a lot easier to be mentally tough." I have believed in being mentally tough especially as a former football player and coach. This verse has gotten me through many challenges in my life. Phil: 4:13 is another one. "I have the strength to face all conditions." This has strengthened me these past months. I tend to get whatever symptoms are told to me. Therefore, I asked to be spared of the knowing the possible symptoms ahead. However, I was told I would be much more emotional after my heart transplant. And that has proven true. God knows what we need. I have tried to pray and thank the Lord for the many blessings I have had and to continue to bless me rather than requesting what I think I need and want. God knows our needs. Another verse I love is I Thes. 5:16-18: "Be joyful at all times…." Put things in God's hands and let Him work it out. I want to say how much I have appreciated this church. He became a bit emotional when saying, "The love and prayers have meant more than you will ever know."

Me: Just speaking today is an answer to prayers as we have prayed to help others in some way from what we have experienced. The prayers for Jack and I seemed limitless. Jack has already been a mentor for a person looking at the possibility of a heart transplant. We have left the ways up to him so here we are. Prayers of people all over: this church, so many others. Personally, I knew I needed strength and peace for what was ahead. Our longtime friend from Danville, Mark Dexter, called as we were waiting for Jack to be taken for the surgery. I asked him to pray for strength for me and he instantly quoted from Jeremiah, "My people can call on my strength in times of need." I hung on tightly to that verse for a very long time. God used Mark to give me strength. When I asked him later where was that verse, he did not remember telling me that or where that verse even was.

I went on to share about the miracles that I knew had happened, our pastor Rob coming at just the right time, my phone call with Marna, the miraculous fact we had built a house in the Charlotte area, the too "thick" blood problem, double the sleep prayer, the beauty of a perfect sinus rhythm, our peaceful wait time and other blessings of steps on God's pathway I have already shared with you in this book. It was so fulfilling to put all of this together and share with a church congregation we loved so much.

I closed with the following: "We do not know God's plan ahead for us. No one does. None of us know that. What we do know is that God has blessed our family with more miracles to fulfill the plan than we could ever imagine. Jack has been healed. He feels better than he has for years. No need for a pacemaker, defibrillator, artificial valve. He is off coumadin which he had taken since 1973 with a blood test once a month or more often if necessary. Looking back, it has been an amazing walk. Jesus has been there every step of the way and held each of our family members tightly. If you have been amazed at our story, maybe you would like to look back at your own life and realize God's presence is in your life and see your pathway."

One other interesting fact about our London church. While Jack was waiting for his heart, Layla Tyler, a toddler there, was waiting for a liver transplant. What are the chances in a church of about 350 people, that two people would need organ transplants? We were more than just church connected to Layla as her mom, Jennifer Tyler, was a very close friend of our daughter's while they were growing up. Thankfully, Layla received her liver transplant before Jack received his heart and is doing super as I write.

August 13: Jack mowed all week and surprisingly was not bothered by the heat at all. People would call or ask me when they saw me if I knew he was out there or if he was allowed. It is so great to live in a town where people know and care about each other.

August 21: Another biopsy. A blood clot had developed in his groin so the doctor went through his neck for the biopsy. Jack described it as rough. The patient is awake for this procedure so you can image how strange it must feel. He scored a 1 on the biopsy. Since there was a blood clot, he was put back on Coumadin. One of the very positive aftermaths of a heart transplant is the possibility to get off Coumadin. Jack had been on it since 1973 and was so glad not to have the monthly blood test to say nothing of the dangers of taking Coumadin. That's a lot of blood tests from Nov of '71 until March 2007. Ouch! So here we were back on it and back on the blood tests.

Email update
From: Jack & Carol Eicher
Sent: Sunday, August 26, 2007 8:19 P.M.
Subject: Jack scores another 1!

Hi to all,

I said in my last email I probably would not send updates as frequently. However, some of you tried and true friends have called or emailed to see how things went last week. I trimmed the list a bit so here goes.

The 1 is another great score, although we are still pulling for the BIG 0! They could not get into Jack's groin and decided to do an ultrasound. They found a blood clot where they had entered so many times. Therefore, he is back on coumadin for awhile. They were successful through the neck, but it was rough. To see the miracle in this did not take long. If they had gone down his neck first and not tried his groin, we would not have known about the blood clot and it could have moved through his body. A bit of danger there! He does not have any restrictions but is not looking forward to the blood tests that go with coumadin. To give the blood clot time to dissolve and since Jack has had such great scores, we do not have another biopsy for 6 weeks!

We received a letter from our donor's family. According to our donor's family, our donor was a very giving young woman in her 30s, active in her community and job and a lover of people. Her family are NASCAR fans and attend the 2 Charlotte races each year. There are also teachers and coaches in her family. We will be forever grateful for her gift to Jack. She was able to donate all of her major organs so several other families feel just as we do.

We are heading to Emily's this week to celebrate Joseph's 3rd B-Day. Jeff, Kim and the twins will be there too. God is good and has blessed us so much!

May each of you see the blessings in your lives as well.

Love to all,
Carol

August 31 – Sept. 3: We left for Emily's after school to celebrate Joseph's 3rd birthday. Every celebration felt like a miracle with Jack there, alive and well.
Life seemed to be back to normal: I was teaching in school and Jack was happy as could be mowing and taking care of his customers.

Sept. 22 & 23: We went to Charlotte to see twins. I missed them bunches after seeing them almost every day while we were there. We rode our bikes in a park there for four miles, all six of us, Jeff, Kim, the twins, Jack and I. Such a fun time.

Sept. 27: We worked at Kentucky Organ Donor Affiliates (KODA) booth at Chicken Festival in London. We were and still are determined to promote organ donation. Are you an organ donor? If not, think about it.

Sept. 28: Met Jeff, Kim and the twins in Gatlinburg. We happily beat the streets and did a bit of hiking. Seemed as though Jack's energy level had no bounds.

Email update
From: Jack & Carol Eicher
Sent: Sunday, October 07, 2007 8:45 P.M.
Subject: Update on Jack: It's all GOOD!

Hi to all,

Jack had a biopsy last Monday. He is back to the BIG 0!!!!! No rejection! We were so excited. He will go off prednisone next week and have another biopsy the last Monday in Oct. He is only taking 2.5 mg now, so we hope that he will continue with 0s after he is off completely. Some patients do fine without it and some continue to take it the rest of their lives. We are praying he will be fine w/o it.

Everything else is going great. Normal, busy life continues. We continue to be blessed in ways we could never have requested from Jesus or imagined. It was great to be back with the twins again when we were in Charlotte for the biopsy. Each time we go back, they ask where we have been and say they have missed us. They are both "playing" soccer and Jeff is one of the coaches. Jesse is more interested in stopping and looking at any bugs that might be visible around him than chasing that ball. I'm sure he will be one of the world's great scientist! Jack is a bit more focused, but not much. There are 3 Jacks on their team so our Jack decided he wanted to be called "Duke." (How about that DeLucas? Duke must have made a great impression on him when you all visited!)

Thank you each again for your interest in Jack's continued remarkable recovery. When we go for the biopsies and have all the questions to answer, the Drs, nurses, and PAs first ask what feat he has accomplished since the last visit. This time he could say he had rebuilt our deck! I can see it could become difficult to keep up with his 30 something heart. Blessings often come in strange ways!

We have joined the new Powerhouse Gym in London. It has been years since Jack could work out and get his heartrate up for an extended period of time. He loves it!

Best go and get ready for the week ahead. One more week and we will have fall break. That is a HUGE blessing!

Take care and love to all,
Carol

Oct. 16, 2007: Stopped Prednisone. This was a huge deal for him.

Oct. 23: Jack received a flu shot as recommended by the heart team. We felt protected but little did we know what was ahead in the name of the flu.

Oct. 29: Biopsy—scored a 0. First one off Prednisone. Took a long time to go in. There was an emergency procedure before us. Medical personnel kept apologizing for the wait. I have never understood why people would be upset on waiting for a doctor that is taking care of a patient in dire need. If I were the person in need, I would want the doctor's undivided, undistracted attention to my situation. Instead of fretting over the wait, I feel compelled to thank the Lord that the person in there is not me or one of my family members. And the next step is to pray for the person being attended to and the doctor in that specific medical procedure. For as you know if you are reading this book, miracles are everywhere.

I stopped by the chapel after they took him to do the biopsy. One chaplain was preaching while another chaplain in there came and spoke to me. He prayed for Jack and Charlie, our great nephew having some kidney issues. I looked at the prayer request list as I was leaving: Von family had requested prayers. It was the beginning of my prayers for someone on the list each time I went.

Email update
From: Jack & Carol Eicher
Sent: Sunday, November 04, 2007 9:09 P.M.
Subject: Good news on Jack

Hello to All,
Jack had a biopsy on Oct 29 and scored a 0!!!!!!!
NO REJECTION!!! This was an important one
due to the fact he had been off Prednisone for 2
weeks. Some patients begin to show rejection
of their transplanted heart after coming off steroids.
Because of this possibility, he will have another
biopsy Oct 13, just 2 weeks after the last one.
However, he is feeling great and not showing any
signs of rejection at this point. We continue to
praise God for the blessings and ask that you do
the same.

We had a beautiful worship service this morning
observing National Donor Sabbath. Our pastor
preached about agape love and giving of
ourselves as Jesus did. Prayers were focused on
those who had received organs and especially on
the families of donors everywhere. It was very
humbling to have Jack there and Layla, a two year
old who received a liver 2 months before Jack
received his heart. Donor Sabbath can be observed
anytime in Nov. Perhaps your church will be doing
so or you can suggest it.

Before I close, I would like to request that you pray
for our new great nephew, Charlie. He was born
last Fri to Megan (Cheri's daughter for those that
know her) and her husband Chuck. He has only

one functioning kidney and is undergoing test at Children's Hospital in Cinti. They knew there were problems before birth so it has been a difficult time for them. He did arrive a whooping 9lb 8oz. He looked very out of place in the neo-natal unit with the itty-bitty babies! They did get to take him home and then take him in for tests. He is their 2nd son. Matt is 3, one month older than our Joseph. Please lift them up in prayer as we hope for another miracle in our family.

Take care, keep in touch and "LOVE ONE ANOTHER"
Carol

Email update
From: Jack & Carol Eicher
Subject: Jack gets another good score!

Hi to all,
Hope everyone had a wonderful Thanksgiving! We are still in MO at Emily's. Planning to leave on Sat. What a thankful day we had! Jack's score last week was a 1. Although we like the 0s better, the drs. were very happy with a 1 since Jack had been off prednisone for 5 weeks. We are also glad to now able to share more family news - Emily and Herb are expecting their 2nd baby! About mid-June. She is feeling fine and Joseph is already making plans to save some of his toys for the baby.

I know several of you on this email list are experiencing difficult times in your families with health issues. Know that we are thinking of you and praying just as you did for us.

We know God listens and answers even if the answers are not exactly what we were expecting. We have been thinking about our donor family this week as it is their 1st holiday season w/o their family member.

Everyone take care and keep your focus on Jesus,
Carol

CHAPTER 10

The Knee Incident – Questioning God's Pathway

Nov. 25: Jack was having some minor cold symptoms. Nothing to be concerned about.

Nov. 26: A routine blood test. Everything seemed normal.

Nov. 27: Jack woke up sick in the night with an upset stomach. We were both thinking it might be food poisoning as we had eaten crab for dinner. We talked with our nurse, Susan. She advised us to watch his symptoms closely.

Nov. 29: Jack was having symptoms of kidney stones. Somehow I knew this was not good. His kidneys were not fully functioning so a bit of fear checked in with me.

Nov. 30: He went to see our London family doctor and was diagnosed with kidney stones. He also was beginning to cough and have mucous.

Dec. 2: By this day, he was not only coughing and sounding very raspy, but was also running a low-grade fever. We spoke with a transplant nurse to keep them posted. My brain was beginning to shift into nurse mode once again.

Dec. 4: After three days with the low-grade fever, it ticked up to 100.9. We kept the transplant center informed and went back to our London family doctor. She diagnosed him with the flu, but thankfully not pneumonia. He started on Tamiflu. What about that flu shot he had gotten?

Dec. 5: The next day he was very sick. He did not get out of bed.

Dec. 6: Jack was still very sick. His temperature was not high, 99.7, but he had terrible pain in his side and back. He begged me to take him to local hospital. The pain and fear were so apparent in his voice. At 10:30 P.M. we went to the hospital in London. His potassium was high and he was dehydrated. An IV was started. He was in a room at 3:30 A.M. Of course, I checked in by phone with transplant nurse, Susan, back in Charlotte. We were in a two-bed room. The man in the next bed kept getting up, even though he was not supposed to. They had his bed alarmed so every time he got up, alarm on his bed alarm would sound. Sort of like a police car in the room. It was a very long night. I so longed to be in Charlotte with the doctor and nurses that would know exactly what to do to take care of Jack.

Dec. 7: The medical staff there decided Jack needed to be airlifted to Charlotte as they were concerned he was having some heart issues along with the flu. So here comes another miracle. At an October meeting of the London Chapter of KODA, we were informed of the medical air transport company, Air Med. We paid to join the next day, not only for Jack, but for me too. If would be my luck to pay for Jack and then I would be the one that needed it one day. When Dr. Shelley Stanko, our family physician, said she would arrange for us to be flown to Charlotte, I told her we belonged to Air Med. I even had my membership card on me. She said that would make it a bunch easier and cheaper. About the cheaper part, that is for sure. Air Med pays for bed to bed, includes the flight and the ambulances. There is no charge to members. I do not know what today's cost would be but at that time, it would have cost us about $20,000.00. It was a miracle we had joined just two months earlier.

To be ready to fly to Charlotte, I had a few things to do. I drove home and packed a few things. Pastor Rob had come to the hospital to check on Jack. He followed me home, I packed a few things while feeling nervous inside. He took me back to the hospital. No car was needed for this trip to Charlotte. When the plane arrived, part of the Air Med medical staff came to Jack's room and prepared him for the ride in a Laurel County ambulance to the London Airport. The team shared with us that they thought it was London, England, when first told they had a call to go to London. They were relieved as they had just completed an international flight the day before. The pilot had food for us when we got on the plane. Eating gave me something to do while we were in the air. Jack was so very sick, but I had no doubt these people were the best at what they did. From the Charlotte Douglas Airport, we went to Carolina Medical Center in an ambulance. I rode in the front and the driver was the same driver that had taken Jack from University Hospital to CMC in 2005. Yes, that is right. She recognized the two of us. I was never so glad to put my feet on Charlotte, NC, soil as that day. I said that to one of the ambulance staff. He said, "I guess you are from here." No I wasn't, but the comfort of being in the same proximity as the transplant medical staff Jack and I had come to love was as much of a feeling of coming home as I have ever experienced. How comforting that God sends people along our path to help give us comfort and peace.

I have only arrived at the hospital by ambulance once before. That was for a car accident and I just needed a few stitches in my head. This was totally different. I was not the one needing medical treatment, but I was so relieved to get there. Carolina Medical Center looked like Disney World to me. Jack was feeling so bad and I knew if anyone could save him, it was the heart transplant team. They were expecting us and he was quickly transported from the emergency room to an ICU room. Members of the transplant team showed up immediately. I don't know how Jack was feeling but I was feeling so much better and thanking God for his presence all the time.

The following email was sent by my wonderful coworker at South Laurel High School.

From: King, Mary
Sent: Friday, December 07, 2007 5:47 P.M.
To: SLHS - Teachers; SLHS - Office Staff; SLHS - Staff; SLHS - Guidance
Subject: Eicher Update

Jack and Carol arrived safely at the hospital in North Carolina. Jack is in ICU. At this time (Friday Night), the doctors do not think it is rejection. He is still fighting the flu and maybe pneumonia.

Mary King
Family and Consumer Science Teacher
South Laurel High School

Dec. 8: Jack was moved to room 6223, the last room on the left. The team had determined he just had the flu, no rejection, no pneumonia. What a relief! We had one logistics issue to solve. We had no car to get back to Kentucky. Jeff and John offered to drive to London and bring the car back to us. They talked a lot in the trip to London. Said they hadn't had that kind of time together for years. God does provide special times for his people in difficult times. Can you think of times like that in your life? One comes to mind for me. When my dad was in his last hours and unconscious, my nephew, Scott, came to sit with his grandpa and me. It was just the two of us and we had such a meaningful time together. I had never had the opportunity to sit and chat with Scott like that before. I realized what a caring young man he is. Although Dad could not participate, there is something in me that believes he knew it was going on and was smiling deep within his soul.

Dec. 9: I was expecting Jack to feel better but he felt terrible. He suffered a gout attack in the night in right ankle. It was so painful, he was given morphine. He was still very sick, complaining of some pain in his chest and back. Said it seemed like sore muscles.

Email update to my best friend in college
Jack & Carol Eicher wrote:

Hi Donna,
I'm writing to you from Charlotte, NC - Jack's hospital bed to be exact. He somehow got the REAL flu, started last Sunday, went to the Dr. Tuesday, appeared to be improving until Thursday evening, he was awful. Went to our local hospital, they put him in a room and by Friday AM, they were concerned he had pneumonia and some fluid around his heart, possibly indicating rejection of the heart. They and <u>we</u> wanted to get to the transplant center, so we were airlifted by AirMed to Charlotte. I was never so glad to get to a hospital in my life! Only took 45 minutes in the air. Anyway, after several tests, the transplant team determined that it was only the flu, no heart damage or rejection. Prayers answered! They may let us out today and we may stay a day or two here and then go back to London. He has had gout before and it flared up

91

really bad last night. I'm not sure what that will do to the schedule. will keep you posted also.

I know how you feel about your team going down the tubes. We thought UK was going to have a great year and they fell apart also. However, they did better than they have in years so that was fun. Tell your mom hi and hope she is feeling well.

Love ya,
Carol

Email update from Mary King
Sent: Monday, December 10, 2007 7:58 A.M.
To: SLHS - Teachers; SLHS - Staff; SLHS - Office Staff; SLHS - Guidance
Subject: Eicher Update

Jack is out of ICU. He does not have pneumonia which is an answer to prayers! They expect to be in the hospital a few more days. They hope to return to London Thursday or Friday.

Mary King
Family and Consumer Science Teacher
South Laurel High School

Dec. 10: Jack was started on colchicine for the gout and a large dose of steroids. Dr. Reames, the surgeon, stopped by to say hi. A rheumatologist came by, checked Jack's ankle and said she would be back in the morning to take some fluid. I stopped by the chapel to thank God for being in Charlotte. I checked the prayer list in the chapel and read a family member had died on their birthday. If you ever want to have reasons to pray for people, just stop by the hospital chapel and read the prayer list. So many needs, broken hearts and a few joys. Little did I know how great our need for prayer would be in the very near future.

Dec. 11: The rheumatologist took fluid from ankle to check for crystals caused by gout. We were released from hospital. We stayed in Moss Creek as a biopsy was scheduled for Thursday, the next day.

Dec. 12: Jack scored a 0 on the biopsy. That was great news as no rejection had occurred because of the flu. He was still feeling wimpy from the flu. The bad news was his potassium was high, he was a bit dehydrated, and his kidney function was not as good as it had been. They gave him an IV and then sent us to our Concord house. The twins came over and I made gingerbread houses with them. A great diversion after what I had been through.

Dec. 15: Fri.: We headed home to London, thinking Jack was on the mend. He was feeling much better, even insisted on driving some. As we were watching TV that evening, he mentioned that his left knee, the artificial one, felt weird, not painful, just strange.

Dec. 15: Sat.: Upon awakening, he felt badly, staying in bed all day with a slight fever. This was not good. A bit of fear crept into my being. By evening, he couldn't put any weight on left knee. His right hand also hurt. We thought it was gout.

Dec. 16: Sun.: Jack woke up with 102 temperature. He could not put ANY weight on his left knee and BOTH hands hurt. We called a nurse on the transplant team and she said to check it out locally. Oh, how I wanted to be back in Charlotte. Dr. Stanko was on call and instructed us to go to the hospital. Remember, he was unable to put any weight on the left knee. We had a walker from when he had the artificial knee implanted. I thought sure he could use that to get to the car. Not a chance!

I had to roll him on an office chair through the house. He hopped down the three steps into the garage on his right leg in great pain. An X-ray was taken at the hospital and an orthopedist was called. He took fluid off the knee and stated it probably needed surgery. However, he would not do the surgery as he had not put the knee in. He recommended we see Dr. E. in Lexington, who had put the knee in. Oh, my! What was ahead for us??? I had to focus on keeping the faith.

Email update
Sent: Sun 12/16/2007 10:07 P.M.
Subject: News and prayer request for Jack

Hi to our friends and family,
To make a long story short, Jack has had a rough weekend. It has been determined that he has an infection in his artificial knee. We will head to Lex tomorrow to see the Dr. that put it in. Please pray for him as he is in lots of pain and cannot walk. Last week he had the REAL flu and we were airlifted to Charlotte. He has had a biopsy and there is no heart damage or rejection through this. God has been so good to us. We are still faithful that through His awesome power, all will be OK. Love to all and thank you for your concerns and prayers.

Take care,
Carol

Dec. 17: Dr. E. drew fluid and then sent us straight to a hospital in Lexington, one of the top orthopedic hospitals in the country. Since we didn't have a local doctor there, Dr. H., an internist, took care of Jack. He could not believe Jack's history. A couple times he even said, "How much more?" Dr. A., a doctor with the orthopedic group, checked in on Jack. Terrible pain continued in his left knee. We were put in a room off from others so Jack would not be exposed to anything else or give the flu to any other patients. I stayed at Rose Sharon's daughter, Angela Bradley's, in Lexington. My heart longed to be in Charlotte, where the transplant team could keep watch over him. Why had we left Charlotte? Just one more day there and we would be in the hospital we loved with the people we had claimed as our new family and miracle workers of God.

Dec. 18: Dr. Stanko called with results from bloodwork and knee fluid. Jack had a strep pneumonia infection in his knee. The strep that follows the flu in the elderly. Since Jack had a suppressed immune system this wasn't surprising but to have it in his knee was quite unusual. Then it was determined that Jack had pneumonia in his lungs. Things were going downhill. This was harder than the heart transplant. Every day was better after the transplant. Now every day was worse. Infectious doctors were also called in to be on Jack's team of doctors. When Dr. E. came that evening, he said he had to go back in and the knee probably had to come out. A spacer would be put in (akin to a block of concrete) for six to eight weeks. That was the usual procedure to make sure all the infection had been eradicated. He would be in a wheelchair unable to walk. Then they would go back in and put in another knee. How much could my Jack endure? Then Dr. E. added we all needed to pray. What a touching moment when he took one of my shaking hands and one of Jack's hands and prayed for Jack, for me and for himself to have steady hands, clarity of mind and for surgery to go without a hitch. It was a mighty moment of God at work in our lives. It gave me strength and peace to know this man was a Christian and knows that God is needed for healing. Seems God had put us in the right place after all.

Dec. 19: Knee surgery was next. Seemed scary to head into surgery with the flu AND pneumonia. I walked as far as they would let me go, gave him a kiss and started to turn to walk to the waiting room. One of the doctor's assistants must have sensed my anxious feelings. He told me Jack was in the best of hands. "Dr. E. is a machine once he starts. No need to worry." That was comforting. I headed to the waiting room, full of unknown people to me. I plopped myself in a corner chair to wait things out. I had brought a *Blue Ridge Country* magazine and was reading it. God spoke to me through a picture in that magazine. A beautiful nature picture. God speaks to us in so many different ways. So often we are not listening. Stop here a minute and think of the ways He has spoken to you. Through friends, sermons, radio, books, music, thoughts? He is all around us, yet often we don't recognize the voice that created us. How frustrating it is to parents when their children don't listen to them, the ones they came from. I believe it might be so with God when we don't listen.

Shortly after the magazine picture, our dear friends Lynn and Steele Harmon surprisingly walked through the room. Can't remember a time I was happier to see them. Lynn, one of those special lifetime friends that I have learned much from—how to be calm, how to accept others, how to open your home to Christian groups. We hugged and then prayed. Time passed so much faster after they came to minister to me. Then, it happened. Dr. E. marched in the room, looked around the crowded room and spotted me. Huge smile on his face, clenching some sort of plastic bag in his hand and said something like, "Here it is!" and handed it to me. He went on to say THE BEST POSSIBLE THING HAD HAPPENED! Since Jack had a suppressed immune system, the infection had spread quickly and caused terrific pain but had not gone into the bone deeply. So, he was able to remove the old metal/plastic knee, shave off the infected knee parts, slather on the antibiotics and insert a new knee. No spacer was necessary; no wheelchair would be needed. I'm not sure who was the happier—the doc or me. He left me with the old artificial knee in one hand, tears on my face and two friends to share the joy. The Lord had granted us another miracle. Seemed we were securely on his pathway for us.

Dec. 20: After a tough night of fever and pain, it was hurting for Jack to breathe. There was fluid on his lungs. While I never doubted Jack would be okay after his heart transplant, there were times during this struggle I thought I would lose him. I tried to keep the faith that all would be okay and he would recover but doubt crept in several times. One of the infectious doctors drained fluid from his lungs. He was given two pints of blood. Lynn, Steele, Grady (my brother) and Kate (our niece) came to visit Jack. Mary and Steve King brought a sunshine basket from South Laurel High School. Lots of dark chocolate! By evening Jack was feeling much better.

Dec. 21: This day brought clear lungs! Much improved. He even walked on crutches. His left lung was sore and inflamed from the liquid-removing procedure, but I was so thankful. Looked like God was going to heal him again. I just kept sending thanks and praise to God. I wonder sometimes how many times God heals us from physical ailments we are not even aware we have. Our immune system is one amazing creation, at work all the time. This was an "in your face" healing. Visible to many. I believe many are not so visible.

Dec. 22: Cheri, my sister, and her husband, Dan, came to visit. Jack was doing very well. He had two tough physical therapy sessions and walked several laps on crutches. While most knee replacements are moving the knee as soon as possible after surgery, he was not able to do that because of the pneumonia. He was getting a later start to recovery. Emily and Herb came to visit. Christmas was getting close. We were supposed to have Christmas in London. It was supposed to be a celebration of Jack's first Christmas with a new heart. Alternate plans would prevail. Couldn't see Joseph, Jackson or Jesse as he was not allowed around kids. This was breaking his heart but he understood for sure.

Dec. 23: Herb, our son-in-law, had a grandmother living in Lexington. Mama Minnie graciously invited us to use her house for our Christmas celebration. Jeff, Kim and the twins came from Charlotte. Emily, Herb and Joseph were coming to Lexington to be with Herb's family for Christmas. Seemed like we would have a Christmas together after all. God is so good. Of course, Jack could not leave the hospital but insisted I leave the hospital and go be with them to eat and open presents. My heart was heavy that he could not see the grandkids but filled with joy that he was going to live. Jeff, Emily, and John went together to see him in the hospital. If you have adult married children, you know it is not often that those adult children are together without their spouses and kids. Kind of special to see just the three of them take off together again. Looked like old times.

Dec. 24: Christmas Eve: To our surprise, Jack was released and we went home to London. John helped us and then he took off to Charlotte.

Dec. 25: Christmas Day: It was a quiet day in London. We were both just so thankful to be there and for Jack to be on the mend. The Great Healer had blessed us once again but the recovery path ahead was not an easy one.

Email update
12-25-07

Hello to all,
I'm writing this on Christmas and thankful to be doing so from our London home. Although our Christmas greeting is a bit late, you will understand after reading this update on Jack. He is doing very well right now. However, it has been quite challenging the past month. Any situation such as this can be quite serious for any organ transplant recipient. You will see God has had his hand upon us once again.

Most of you already know that Jack had a kidney stone, followed by the flu & fever at which time we were airlifted from London to the Carolina Transplant Center where we stayed for a week. They released him with no signs of pneumonia and sure he was on the way to recovery. We even stayed 2 extra days in NC while they did a routine biopsy with a resulting 0 - No Rejection, after all he had been through! However, the day after we got home, Jack's artificial knee (inserted in Jan 2005) hurt so bad, he could not put any weight on it. Off to the emergency room we went where it was determined that there was an infection in his knee which needed quick attention. We headed to Lexington on Monday to Dr. E who had put the knee in in '05. After only 5 minutes in the office and drawing fluid from his knee (that really hurt), the Dr. told us that Jack would be admitted right away and a scope would be done that afternoon by the 1st Dr. that could get to him. The scope and culture showed that he had strep pneumonia growing the artificial joint. They had never seen that bacteria grow on an artificial joint before. So on Wed they did a total knee replacement. We were expecting the Dr. to put in a temporary concrete spacer (that's right, concrete)which stays in place for 6-8 weeks and has medicine to bathe the area. (Leg straight, no weight on the joint, yuck!) Then a new knee is inserted. However, he was able to put in a new knee b/c it had happened so fast due to Jack's suppressed immune system that the infection had not spread far into the bone. I'm not sure who was the most excited - me or the Dr.! God had once again granted us a miracle we didn't even ask for or know was possible. By the way, Dr. E does not work on Wed but came in to do Jack's surgery. He prayed with us on Tuesday night after telling us replacement had to be done the next day. The day after surgery, pneumonia did show up on the chest X-ray and fluid began to fill Jack's lungs that night. The fluid was drawn out and no infection was there. Yeah - PTL!

When we 1st got to Lexington, we were both wishing we had stayed in NC close to the heart drs. However, we soon found out, it is always best to have the Dr. that put in the original knee do the surgery if an infection appears. It seemed that God had put us in the right place again. St. Joe's is one of the top hospitals in the country for orthopedics. We came home on Christmas Eve day with a normal white blood count (yeah), a machine for Jack's knee, a pic line for me to insert medicine each day for 8 weeks and Dr. appointments for follow up. But with thankful hearts that there was only one type of infection present and it was curable. Thanks to all of you for your continued prayers, phone calls and well wishes. A special thank you to Lynn and Steele who seemed like angels to me when they appeared at the hospital. Please continue to pray. Jack has a way to go yet before he is well. His blood and hemoglobin are low and he does not have much energy. However, that is not surprising considering what he has been through. Also pray that the infection will not reappear.

A couple last thoughts for those of you wondering. Our 3 children and their families were all together on Sunday in Lexington to celebrate Christmas. We had plans to all celebrate in London this year. Herb has a grandmother with a large house in Lex which we took over Sunday afternoon. Jack. of course, could not join us and was unable to see the grandsons (he is restricted from being around children for awhile) but it was a blessing to have them together. I stayed at Angela Hunt Bradley's home while in Lex which was such a positive in a scary situation. God does provide for His children during our times of need!

Love to each of you and be looking for the blessings around you and your loved ones. They are there even in the most difficult of times.

Carol & Jack

Dec. 26: We once again had a home nurse. But for a different purpose. This home nurse was also a physical therapist.

Dec. 27: At Dr. D.'s, the infectious doctor, I learned to give an IV through Jack's PIC line. I felt sure I would be given my RN degree before the training was over. Jack still needed to be pumped with antibiotics to make sure the infection was totally gone from his knee. Occasionally he was still running a low-grade fever. As we look back, it was the infectious doctors and Dr. E. that saved Jack's life this time. We ate at Frisch's after the appointment. We went through the drive-thru as Jack was in back seat with leg straight out and it seemed too overwhelming to get out of the car. Jack and I grew up with Frisch's food. That was one of our teenage hangouts in our hometown of Ft. Thomas, Kentucky. Not sure why, but that Big Boy might be the best Big Boy I ever had.

Dec. 28 & 29: His knee was sore, giving us two rough days. The white compression socks he had to wear made his knee even more sore. Fevers in evening.

Dec. 30: Best day yet.

Dec. 31: New Year's Eve: Dr. E. in morning for post-op check. The knee looked great, no more brace! He then said, "You were a tough one. It took prayer to know what to do." So how about that. A doctor that has done hundreds, maybe thousands of knee surgeries (he only does hips and knees) still relies on the Lord to give him instructions in surgery. So maybe each of us need to ask the Lord each day for directions at work or home even if we've done the job a thousand times. And it was good that we left Charlotte before the knee infection. Another look back on the pathway. God watches us and puts us just where we need to be in His plan. Are you where God wants you?

We were about to embark on a New Year 2008. We both felt optimistic. God had been with us every step of the way. Sometimes we didn't realize it until after the event. Seems that happens often. It's not until we look back and say, "Oh, that is why that happened and I am better for it. Thank you, Jesus!"

Jan. 1, 2008: Good day.
IV seems to make his temperature rise.

Jan. 2, 2008: PT visit, lungs seems worse.

Jan. 3, 2008: Dr. R., another infectious doctor, seemed concerned about fever each night.
Hemoglobin 8.9, way too low.

Jan. 10, 2008: Dr. R. stopped Coumadin for upcoming biopsy.

Jan. 11, 2008: We were scheduled to see Dr. M., a blood specialist, in Charlotte at 10:15 A.M. There was a storm the night before and we were both too tired to go in the rain. I was still doing all the driving. We decide to go to bed early and left London at 3:30 A.M. to get there. We made it on time but I was wiped out the rest of the day.

Jan. 13, 2008: Went to the Newhearts Support Group meeting. It was good to be on the mend and everyone was so glad to see Jack. He received two pints of blood @ the Blood Center. Jack felt guilty getting blood others might need. We were so ready to do something non-medical that we went to a stamp show in Charlotte. Jack is a stamp collector.

Email update
From: Jack & Carol Eicher
Sent: Saturday, January 19, 2008 9:08 A.M.
Subject: Jack scores another 0!!!!!

Hi and Happy New Year to All,
Hope this finds each of you in good health. Jack had a biopsy on Monday and in spite of all his body has been through in the last 6 weeks, there was no heart rejection!!!!! The transplant team was thrilled. He is continuing to improve each day - can drive again, goes to therapy for his new knee, works out at the Powerhouse Gym and is enjoying some renewed energy. He is still anemic after blood transfusions, but a blood specialist is working to find the cause. The knee recovery is a slow process as we remember from the 1st one in Jan '05. Thank goodness it is not mowing season. God's timing is awesome! The strep pneumonia bacteria is no longer in the blood stream so they hope to remove the pic line about the 2nd week of Feb. By then I should have enough medical infusion hours to be a "specialist." HA!

Thank you again for all your prayers and concerns. This last month has been more difficult than the time surrounding the heart transplant. Many organ transplant recipients do not survive pneumonia so we are very thankful for the healing that has and continues to take place. We thank God for you and your prayers!

Take care and keep praying for <u>all of those you love</u>. Jack is a miracle that proves prayer brings results!

Love to all,
Carol

Jan. 24, 2008: Dr. M. called Dr. R.—wants Jack on Progrit to help hemoglobin. When my parents both were fighting physical ailments, my mom would say, "Our social life is going to the doctor and then going out to eat." I felt we were getting there.

Jan. 27: Went to Cumberland Falls for lunch—beautiful. Everything seemed more beautiful than before this knee trauma. The Falls seemed more amazing than ever before and I had looked at them many times. Funny how the same things can look different after experiences in our lives. If you have never been to Cumberland Falls near Corbin, Kentucky, put it on your list to do. It is one of America's treasures.

Jan. 27: Appointment with Dr. E. to check Jack's knee. He was pleased and glad Jack had pulled through. He did not have to come back for a month! Remember when I said I was afraid I would lose Jack during this time? The doctors' comments, especially Dr. E.'s, confirmed my thoughts. Jack had been very sick with a big chance of not pulling through. But God had plans and blessed us with miracles galore during that time.

Jan. 30: Procrit arrived in mail. The medicine came to us but we took it to the doctor to get the shot.

Jan. 31: Dr. R. again.
Hemoglobin was up to 9.3. He claimed that was a miracle from week before. He gave Jack a shot of Procrit Blood test in a week.

Feb. 3: Jack went back to church. Friends surrounded us as we entered, Jack was still using a walker. Rev. Rob always commented on how glad he was to see him. We even went to Berea, Kentucky, and ate at PapaLeno's. Things were beginning to be a bit more normal, although almost everything made him tired.

Feb. 7: Dr. R. and a second shot of Procrit.

Feb. 9: Back to Charlotte.

Feb. 11, Mon.: Biopsy 0, I was concerned he may have rejection with all he had been through infections, flu, pneumonia, medicines.

Feb. 12: Back to London.

Email update

Hello to All, 2-13-08
Great news from our last biopsy on Monday - another 0. Everyone is thankful after all he has been through since Dec 1. Jack is feeling better as his hemoglobin is coming back up. His knee is still very sore but the surgeon said that is to be expected due to the type surgery that had to be performed. He is close to being back to himself! Thank you for all your prayers.

Our great nephew, Charlie, got super news last week on his kidney and bladder problems. Surgery is still scheduled at 9 months. Keep those prayers going for him also.

There is POWER in PRAYERS!

Take care,
Carol

Feb. 14: Dr. R. appointment, prescribed Amoxicillin to keep any infections in check.

Feb. 22: We wanted to see Joseph, our grandson, so badly. We drove to Emily's in Cape Girardeau and stayed a couple days. There had been an ice storm in western and central Kentucky a couple days before. Ice still covered many trees and trees down all over. It was an amazing drive.

Feb. 25: Emily called. Herb woke up sick in the morning had the flu. This was not good news for Jack. He was started on Tamiflu right away.

March 1, 2008: We went to our 40th high school class reunion in northern Kentucky. It was great! People were so surprised at how great Jack looked. Many knew about the heart transplant but not about the knee.

March 2: My sister, Cheri, had a surprise heart birthday party with a heart-shaped cake. Jack's heart birthday was two days away. We had much to be thankful for.

March 4: One-year heart birthday!!!!

March 14: We drove to Charlotte for his one-year check and another biopsy. I just knew it would be great, another 0, since he was feeling so good.

March 15: Jeff, Kim, and twins came for dinner that Saturday. It was a great day. Jack played ball with the twins, they roughed him up, the house was filled with loud male voices and giggles and screams of delight from two little boys that hadn't seen that from their Papa before. I was overcome with emotion as I watched this event. It was as if we had turned back the years and he was roughing up our boys. "I'm gonna rough you up." An expression that was an almost everyday phrase in our home as Jack would come home from a day full of teaching and coaching other people's children at school. But here we were years later with a fresh heart beating in Jack, recovered from the flu and pneumonia and still in therapy for a second artificial knee. My Jack of old had returned. I quietly thanked God for a miracle such as this.

March 17: He had the one-year biopsy, a cath, EKG, and a chest X-ray. We were not sure what to expect. I expected another 0 or a 1 at worst. As we left the recovery room, we waved and I said, "We'll see you in three months to the nurses." Jack said, "You better not be so sure." But he felt so good and after our great day with the twins, why shouldn't I be so positive?

March 18: We got the call from the nurse. A score of 2.5. Jack was having rejection of his heart. My own heart sank. Even the nurse seemed sad as she spoke. Jack was put on 100 mg of Prednisone daily. Unfortunately, a 2.5 meant we would do a biopsy once a month. Seems he was not out of the woods just yet.

March 23: We were lowering the Prednisone each day by ten less each day. I thought we were to quit after one day of ten. I was so wrong.

March 24: Went to Dr. E. to check up on the knee. All went great. Dr. E. said it was an answer to prayer. Research is now saying to do what Dr. E. did with Jack: put in a new knee rather than the concrete block. It is awesome how God takes care and gives knowledge to men who seek His counsel. Remember, Dr. E. had prayed to know what to do in surgery for Jack. He gave him the answer before the research report had come out. Don't you just love the way God works?

Email update

Hi to all, 3-27-08

I'm a bit late getting this out. Jack had his yearly check up on March 17. Everything came out super - EKG, cath, lung X-ray, blood work and no blood clots. Everyone said he looked his best ever and his exercise tolerance is awesome. We said "bye" to the transplant staff with a "see ya in 3 months." So we were VERY surprised when the nurse called the next day to say he was having moderate rejection, a 2.5 score. He has not had any symptoms at all and still feels great. They put him on Prednisone for 2 weeks to stop the rejection and we headed back to merry old London. We head back to NC this weekend for a biopsy on Monday and will have to wait for the results on Tuesday before we can head back to London. Pray for a 0!!!! We feel all is well and are thankful this was caught before any symptoms showed or heart damage was done. It is still all so awesome to have passed Jack's 1 year heart birthday. The Lord has blessed us with a year beyond belief and understanding. We thank you for taking the journey with us.

On another topic, I have begun to tell people at school that I will be retiring as of July 1 this year. It will be tough to leave a place and the people that I have loved and felt such a part of for 20 years. The hardest part is leaving the Career and Tech people, especially Mary and Bethani, my very 1st and last student teachers. Who in their careers has an opportunity to work with the 2 best they've ever had and trained? It has been great and so rewarding! But it is exciting and peaceful to know that through prayer and an awareness of God's plan for Jack's and my life, it is time to go. Jack and I are excited about what the Lord has in store for us. We are facing the future with faith & with Jesus in heart & hand, knowing there is a path ahead because we've had the opportunity to see the one behind so clearly!

Several of you receiving this are suffering from many different things. While I best not address each one here, please know that we are holding you and your family up in prayer. God's peace to each of you.

Take care and love to all,
Carol

March 31: Another biopsy. Result 1, much better. He was put back on Prednisone for ten more days at 10. I was not supposed to stop it when I did. Oh, my!

Email update
4-01-08

Hi to all,
We are back in London. We are **VERY** thankful that he received a 1 on his biopsy on Monday. Looks like we are back on track again after the moderate rejection 2 weeks ago. He will stay on a low dose of prednisone for awhile and will have another biopsy before too long. We are awaiting a phone call to give us the date to return.

True to his philosophy of life and work ethic and since he had no symptoms of rejection, he continued to work as usual during these past 2 weeks. Lawn work went on, bathroom remodeling in London continued, workouts at the gym went on. When we got to NC, he and John worked all day Saturday on the fence in our backyard that the 2 of them and Jeff had started 2 weeks earlier. What a man! I knew it would tough to keep up with him with a thirty something heart. :)

Thank you again for your prayers! We continue to be thankful and amazed.

Love to all,
Carol

CHAPTER 11

Normal Life on God's Pathway

April 1 - April 19: Jack continued Prednisone.

April 6: Spring Break for Laurel County Schools.
We drove to Charlotte.

April 8-10: We went to Myrtle Beach for a beach getaway.
Saw our wonderful friends Carl and Marcia that live in the area.
On the 10th we rode bikes ten miles in Huntington Beach State
Park. I experienced one of my few falls on my bike while looking
at an alligator in water. No injuries!

April 11: Back in Charlotte for another visit with Dr. M. for
bloodwork. Jack's white count was not yet as high as he wanted it.

April 12: We took the long way back to London through Blowing
Rock, NC. Love that little mountain town. Wanted to stop at
Cabin Fever, one of our favorite stores for log cabin living.
Although we do not live in a log cabin, our North Carolina home

has the atmosphere of one. We had lunch at Knights, a local restaurant there. Ran into one of our friends from our class at Grace Covenant. We were so excited to see him as he was us. He was so glad to see Jack enjoying life once again.

Each and everything we did and everywhere we went, I was just overwhelmed with thankfulness that Jack was alive, with me and getting better every day. I could not say thank you enough to God. What Jack had come through and endured had blessed us beyond my imagination.

April 19: Jack rode in Red Bud Ride 20 miles in London. Another amazing feat for him. The Red Bud Ride is a bicycle ride through the beautiful countryside of London. Kentucky and Laurel County. I volunteered with the Red Bud so I was not riding that day. The area is located on top of the Cumberland Plateau and in the foothills of the Appalachian Mountains. In other words, there are lots of hills. It was tough for me to see him ride off on his bike and not be with him. I was at a checkpoint deep into the ride and kept watching for him to come. Seemed as if everybody had come by my checkpoint. Where was Jack? My thoughts imagined all that could go wrong for him while I kept trying to focus on my job to do. After many riders went by, there he was, visible pumping up the hill, looking great and even smiling as he saw me. Rode by me, saying he was doing great. I was so relieved. And many more riders came after him. Another accomplishment for Jack on God's pathway.

May 5: Biopsy: 0 rejection.
Prednisone dropped to five daily.

June 9: Biopsy: 0 rejection.
Dr. Frank did the biopsy using ultrasound. Now that is common practice.
Still on Prednisone – lowered to 2.5.

Email update
6-10-08

Hi to all,
Jack scored a 0 on his biopsy on Monday! Emily had Anna Carol on June 3. She is a doll. I know some of you already know about Anna, but it doesn't hurt to hear good news twice! She was a bit early but she is in great health. She weighed 5 lb 15 oz, 18 " long.

We have been on the road between MO and NC the past week all for good stuff so there is no complaining, not even on the price of gas. Just thankful we can go and Jack is with me to go. Seeing him hold Anna on her 1st day of life was a miracle to behold. I am heading back to MO tomorrow, Wed, to stay with Emily, Herb, Joseph and Anna for a few days. They will be moving to Chicago at the end of August for Herb's next assignment. Looks like some more travel in our future!

Better go and pack again. Remember to be looking for the miracles in your life. They are there!

Love to all,
Carol

June 21, 2008: We rode 30 miles on the Virginia Creeper Trail, 15 in and 15 out. Awesome and amazing for Jack! One of the places we love. This trail was the first place we rode our bikes on a rail-trail. John was thirteen years old and took a friend. Fourteen miles up. While my legs were killing me and barely functioning, it opened a whole new world to us. Rails to trails give people places to ride bikes with no fear of traffic, beautiful scenery, bits of history and only slight grades. We have since been to many places in the USA to ride the rail-trails.

We continued seeing the infectious doctors and always received a great report. God was and is so GOOD!

July 8: Drove to Charlotte.

July 9: Another biopsy, another 0!
While Jack was having the biopsy procedure, I stopped in the chapel and read the prayer list. I had started stopping at the chapel each time Jack had a biopsy. I would read the prayer requests and pick one on which to focus. Of course, I would hold Jack up in prayer first and then say prayers for those I felt the Lord had put on my heart. My dear friend, Lois Martin, once said, "The Lord puts people on your heart because they need you and He selected you to fulfill their need. If you don't follow up, then he moves on to someone else to help them." Ever since then, I have tried to contact the person who comes to my mind. It is amazing how many times that person was thinking about me!!! I call that ESP miracles through the Holy Spirit. On this day, a family had signed in for prayer and had lost a family member. The deceased's sister wrote in the prayer book that her sister was at peace and how glad she was her sister was at peace. The writer was also in peace. The miracle of the peace of Jesus! We as Christians are so blessed to have the peace of Jesus available to us. He promised.

July 11: We picked up our grandson, Joseph, from his other grandparents'.

July 12: Some of the greatest blessings of Jack's extended life due to the generosity of a person to give all of themselves to anyone in need of lifesaving organs has been time with grandchildren. This was one of those days. There is something special about having grandchildren with you without their parents. They call your name, not their parents' when they have something to say or have a need. We were to take Joseph back to his parents the next day. We decided to take a detour and spend the day at Dollywood with Joseph. He was excited about all that Dollywood had to offer. Jack and I felt so blessed to have him all to ourselves and to watch his wonder and excitement all day. Of course, we did have to tell Emily and Herb that we would not have him back on the planned day but on the next one. To this day, we have been accused of "kidnapping" Joseph for a day.

July 15: We spent our summer vacation in Gatlinburg and the Smoky Mountains National Park.

July 16: Bike ride in Greenbrier area.
Jack forgot to take his medications for the first but not the last time. I have always found that once I feel better from an illness, it's easy to forget to take medications that were prescribed to cure me. I figured that was what happened to Jack that day. He truly was feeling good and healthy. We both sort of panicked but remembered we were told what to do in case that happened. Rejection would not set in immediately. Big sigh of relief.

July 17: Hiked the Gatlinburg trail—four miles.

July 18: Hiked to Greenbrier School in Metcalfe Bottoms.

July 19: Hiked near Clingman's Dome.
Biked the Gatlinburg Trail.
An active vacation for sure, my Jack seemed to be back to himself.

July 24: Taken off prednisone!!!!

Aug. 3: Biked Cove Lake in TN, five miles.

Aug. 5: Biopsy: 0.
Infectious doctors took him off Bactrim.

Aug. 20: Biopsy: 0.
Next one, not for three months!

Email update
8-26-08

Hello to all,
I am so glad to report that Jack received a 0 on his biopsy last week. He does not have to go for another biopsy for 3 months! We are extremely grateful, especially him. While we are not complaining, he has had about 20 biopsies since his transplant in March of 07. He is happy to have a break! We look forward to trips to NC.

Hi again,
Through the magic of technology, the 1st email sent itself before I was done. So here is the rest.

We look forward to trips to NC w/o a hospital visit. He is feeling great. We went on a 32-mile bike ride on a rail-trail Sunday. He was fine - barely broke a sweat. I am still recovering! It must be the 30 something year old heart. :-)

To update everyone on some family news:

Emily and Herb have moved to Naperville, IL, outside of Chicago. Their house is 3 minutes from Nancy Huber's, for those of you that remember them. (I am so sorry to say Bill Huber passed away about 2 months ago - leukemia). We will be heading there this weekend to help get them settled. Tough to move with a 4 yr old and a 3 mo old. <u>A note to all of you Flynns</u> - hope to see more of you now that Emily is close to you.

The twins started kindergarten today - hard to believe! Jeff and Kim are joyful!

John has built a house and will get in it Thursday. Our nephew, Mike, has been transferred to Charlotte and lives with John. It is amazing how the Lord can bring people together. Mike and John were both so sad when we left Ft. Thomas for London. They were both in 1st grade, lived a street apart and were so close. Now they are together again!

Also, I did not actually retire, just switched jobs. I am now with EKU as an assistant grant director for GEAR UP. Won't take your time to explain it all, just know that God gives us wonderful gifts when we least expect them!

Better go. Love to all,
Carol

Sept. 15, 2008: Dr. E., the knee surgeon, gave Jack a good report. Dr. E. was as excited as we were. Return in six months.

Oct. 13: Saw the infectious doctors. Return in six months also. God was slowly moving us to a normal life.

Nov. 19, 2008: Biopsy: 0.

Email updates
11-25-08

Hello to All,

Jack had a biopsy on Nov 19th and scored a 0. It was a very smooth process this time. Our next one is Feb 26th, which will serve as his 2 year checkup. If it is a 0, we will begin having them every 6 months. Believe it or not, we are coming up on 2 years, March 4. He is feeling and looking great, working full time everyday. We feel so blessed! Of course, with the approach of each holiday, our thoughts turn to our donor family. Even though we do not know them, we feel so connected. We were wanting to begin the process of possibly meeting them, but have been told it is too soon. So, we will pray for them and hold the hope that someday the meeting will occur.

Enough about us. We wish each of you a wonderful and blessed Thanksgiving. Look around, be aware. Blessing are all around, some so evident and some in hiding!

Take care
Carol

_____

1-8-2009

Hi to Everyone,
Hope everyone is well. Some special thoughts to send your way for the day: This is Jack's 60th birthday. How amazing, as without <u>God's amazing plan</u> and the gift of science in the hands of dedicated doctors and other medical personnel, he shouldn't be with us anymore. My thoughts are with our donor's family and their generous gift as well as celebrating Jack's remarkable day.

Remember to appreciate and love those that surround you and continue to be looking for your blessings!

Love to All,
Carol

2-27-09

Hi to All,

0 rejection, wide open heart arteries (sometimes these begin to block at the 2-year checkup), clear lungs, great valves and excellent heart pumping power! Couldn't ask for better. <u>We are so blessed</u> that Jack received such a great heart from his donor. He continues to work hard to keep it in such good shape. Thanks to those spinning classes.

Keep looking for those blessings in your life!
Take care,
Carol

9-30-09

Hello to All,
It has been 6 months since I sent my last email with results of a biopsy. Jack had one this past Monday and scored a 0 - No rejection of his heart! He continues to do great, working everyday, keeping those lawns looking great in Laurel County.

Our next big event will be the birth of Emily and Herb's 3rd child. It could be any day as Emily is showing signs of being very close to delivery. We are excited and feeling thankful & blessed that Jack is here to see "No Name Yet Baby Boy." At least we don't know the name yet. They have kept the names of the other 2 secret until the birth.

John has gotten engaged since I've written last. We will be welcoming Christina Burleson into our family. We have loved her from the first meeting :)

They have not set their wedding date yet. Need to find a non-NASCAR weekend in the future!

Hope all is well with you and your families. We know some of you are struggling with health and personal issues. Know our prayers are with you.

Take care and remember to look for the blessings,
Carol

1-13-2010

Hi to Everyone,
Jack and I have taken the BIG step and moved to the Charlotte area! We moved some big "stuff" Monday, finally arriving at our house under the cloak of darkness. Felt sort of like a gypsy! Although we are going to claim this as our base, we will still be in London very frequently as we both have "work" there and we still have our house.

It has been very difficult to leave London after 21.5 wonderful and fulfilling years. That is the longest either of us have been anywhere in one house, including our childhood days. For those of you who have been a part of the Eicher's life during those years, thank you SOOO much! We moved there and claimed London as our home, declaring no more moves to uproot our children. What a wonderful decision that was. The Lord gave us specific directions on that one. :) From our many experiences with the Laurel County Schools, 1st Christian Church and the London Community, the blessings are much too deep to count. We are just thankful to have lived there.

For those of you not in London, we love you and will continue to keep in touch.

Please come and see us in Charlotte! You are always welcome!

Love to All,
Carol & Jack

4-2-10

Hello to All and Happy Easter,
Just a quick note to say Jack came through great at his 3-year checkup. 3 years is a huge milestone with heart transplants so we are really thankful. He scored his usual 0 on the biopsy, has wide open arteries and passed the EKG and 2D Echo with flying colors. Blood results were good also. It was a long day for him but we are always thankful to

be at Carolina Medical Center with such awesome doctors to say nothing of the fact that he is alive to be able to be tested. :)

Thanks to each of you for your prayers, thoughts and well wishes as we have walked this path together. May God bless each of you and your families. Know that we think of those of you that are in rough places right now. May God uphold you and give you peace in your struggles.

Take care and keep looking for the blessings, Carol

CHAPTER 12

Meeting the Donor Family - The Pathway Continues with Blessings

July 21, 2012
CMC Hospital: Heart Transplant Clinic

Feeling nervous, excited, but absolutely ready to meet the donor's family, I was unable to sit still in that waiting chair. Jack, being filled with such a thankful heart for his donor, seemed calmer than me as he always is. But deep down, he was filled with anticipation and the same feelings I was experiencing. We were the first ones there as I refused to be late for this life-changing event. We sat in the waiting area, looking first for Cherie, the social worker with the heart transplant team, as we knew she would be with us and was instrumental in setting up this much-anticipated meeting. Would I say the right words to convey our thankfulness for the gift our donor had given to Jack? Right words? There were none that could express the amount of thankfulness that comes with a successful heart transplant. No words to explain the feeling of knowing God was working his miracles for years behind us, in us and in our future. We would get to meet the mother of our precious donor in the next few minutes. Soon Cherie arrived and took us into a room with chairs circling the perimeter, said a few encouraging words and then it happened. In walked the family we had longed to meet and say thank you for five years and four months. The Donate Life social worker and Cherie attempted to introduce all of us, but they could not talk fast enough to beat Jack and Joyce (mother of Mandy) from an embrace that may be one of the longest in history. Both just broke down in tears while they held tightly to each other. Of course, the rest of us joined in the shedding of tears. It was a few moments in time of a picture that will forever be in my mind's eye and I can pull up at any time. It is as precious as any in my mind. For Joyce to once again to be close to Mandy's heart was so comforting to her.

We had no idea of Mandy's age when we walked into the meeting. We knew Jack had a woman's heart but that was it. We had figured that out from a couple of letters we had exchanged early after the transplant. I so wanted to put a face with that generous lady that had not only given Jack a second life, but also given me the gift of time with him. Joyce brought a picture of Mandy and we brought a picture of our entire family at that time. I am blessed to say the number of grandchildren has grown since then. It was so good to put a face with the gracious woman who had given Jack the gift of life without any idea who would receive her healthy heart. There she was in picture form looking at me with that contagious smile and a generous spirit that jumped right out at me. Somehow, in one of God's miracles, Mandy's spirit was right there with all of us, happy to see her sweet mom finally feeling peace about her early passing by seeing Jack with all his thankfulness just busting right out of his body. They also brought other members of their family with them that day. We were so glad to meet them also.

While there is a process which takes quite a bit of time for the donor's family and the recipient of an organ to come together and meet, we have found it to be well worth the time and effort. We have been so richly blessed to meet and become friends with Joyce and Kenny, Mandy's stepdad. We continue to have a friendship with them. All three of our children and their families have met them. For Joyce, it has given her a peace about the sudden loss of her daughter in a car accident. For her to know Jack is living a full, healthy and very blessed life, it gives her joy amidst her continuing grief. Many of the heart recipients in our support group have not had the opportunity to meet their donor's family. While it has been such a continuing positive experience for Joyce, Kenny and us, there are so many factors on both sides of the story that go into making that face-to-face meeting a reality: circumstances of the death of the donor, age of the donor or recipient, feelings toward the transplant process, distance and just outright fear. One of the emotions that I was not expecting from our meeting and becoming friends with Joyce and Kenny was grief. I have learned much about Mandy over the years and treasure Joyce as a friend like none can ever be. When Jack's heart birthday rolls around each year, it is a joyful time but there is also a grieving for Mandy. It is difficult to understand how this can be but other recipients' wives tell me they feel the same, even if they have not met the donor family. Amazing how God created us to care and feel for others. Jesus felt all human emotions so he understands all of this.

To this day, we have a wonderful relationship with Joyce and Kenny. We get together for dinner when we can. They have even joined us at some of our support group events. The donor families are so welcomed and loved at these events. And yes, Joyce listens to her daughter's heart beating within Jack's chest when we are together. For both families, it has been beyond wonderful to be connected.

Jack's Service on God's Pathway
Considering how many possible life-ending events Jack has been through, he is an amazing waking, talking miracle. If we go back to his college days when his strep throat/rheumatic fever was undiagnosed, it is remarkable he has had an adult life on earth at all. And yet his adult life has touched many lives in positive ways. His years as a winning high school football coach, math teacher and guidance counselor helped more students than I can count. As with any dedicated teacher/coach, we will never know the

positive ripple effects on those many young people. At least not here on earth. During many of those years, he was the Huddle Leader for the Fellowship of Christian Athletes (FCA). We were blessed to take about ten to fifteen high school football players each year to FCA Camp at the Blue Ridge Assembly in Black Mountain, NC. I count those weeks as some of the greatest of my life. They changed the path of my Christian walk, helping me to mature and come closer to Jesus. I can only imagine what it did for those young men. **"Work hard and do not be lazy. Serve the Lord with a heart of devotion" (Romans 12:11, GNB).**

However, I do want to focus on Jack's time after his heart transplant, his second life, as heart transplant recipients call it. His situation as a heart transplant recipient was different from the other three surgeries and his strep throat/rheumatic fever. It was medically possible that death could have taken him because of those events. But waiting for the transplant, well, that was different. Death was a sure thing if a heart did not become available. But thankfully, oh, so thankfully, death did not come at that time and his life continued. Jack has always been a generous and giving person so the fact that he took on some service projects to serve the Lord and say thank you for life is not surprising. Our church, Grace Covenant, offers many opportunities to become the hands and feet of Jesus and share his unconditional love with others. Shortly after we permanently moved to NC, our church had a movement referred to as Servolution. Sunday messages were focused around serving the Lord. As a part of this focus, many different community projects were offered to serve the Lord in or near our community. I served at Samaritan's Feet, an organization where shoes are matched and packaged to ship to those in countries where most people, especially children, have no shoes. I went one time during Servolution. I was fascinated with the program, enjoyed my time there, but have not returned. But Jack's experience was different and life changing. Habitat for Humanity was a choice to serve the Lord in the community. He selected to serve with Habitat, felt in his heart that God put him there (remember that fact) and has continued to this day to help build houses in our area. He was awarded Volunteer of the Year one year and recently was awarded the Golden Hammer Award, the highest honor bestowed on a volunteer. We made an interesting discovery after meeting our donor's family. A Habitat for Humanity home was built in memory of our donor, Mandy Martin, in South Charlotte! Remember the above fact about Jack feeling God wanted Habitat to be his place of service? Mandy's house was sponsored by the company that employed her. That is a fact that might give one chills. I know it did her mom, along with some tears, when we shared that Jack had been volunteering with Habitat since shortly after his transplant of Mandy's heart.

"There are different ways of serving but the same Lord is served" (I Corinthians 12:5, GNB).

Another way Jack has served has been on mission trips to The Sonshine Center in Linefork, Kentucky. One of the Sundays in church shortly after we had made our move to Concord, the church bulletin had opportunities for mission trips that year. One was Linefork, Kentucky. We were baffled that neither one of us had ever heard of Linefork after all those years we had lived in several towns in Kentucky, especially London in southeastern Kentucky. I thought I knew of most every city in eastern Kentucky as our football team had played just about everywhere in those gorgeous mountains, I watched the Mountain News for years, and had met many people from many different Kentucky towns. But no recollection of Linefork. I would like to say here that even though I grew up as a city girl, I came to love the mountains of Eastern Kentucky. I used to tell my mom I was a country girl at heart. It started when I went to Western Kentucky University and met people from all over the state—from farms, small towns, big cities. The Lord opened my heart to different lifestyles than I had grown up believing was the best.

Jack researched the mission work to be done at Linefork, prayed some and decided he wanted to go. Yet I had no desire whatsoever to go. I thought it would be a great opportunity for him to go somewhere without me. He was healthy once again. As many of you probably already know, being a caregiver to someone in poor health attaches you to them in a way that is hard to explain. You are conscious of their every move and feel responsible for keeping them as well as possible. So it was with Jack and me. Not only while waiting for the transplant but afterwards. I watched for symptoms that might merit a call to the transplant team, monitored the taking of medicine, ensured walking was done and kept track of just about anything that seemed important on my medical paper calendar. We were together ALL THE TIME. When this opportunity for him to go away and do something without me occurred, I thought it was perfect. I had to do a bit of talking and convincing him before he agreed to go without me. It was hard to watch the mission team drive away so early that morning but deep down I knew it was another part of his recovery pathway to a normal life. So off he went with the mission team to The Sonshine Center in Linefork. The wonderful people at The Sonshine Center have since come to know and expect his beautiful smile as he has gone many times since that first trip. He has used his landscaping talents while there to prepare the grounds for the summer or winter depending on when the team went. But the real difference he has made has been the relationships he has built with the young men and boys that live there. It is about basketball hoop shooting, talks while sitting on an ancient log, or eating a meal together. It is about the joy in their eyes when they see him return for another few days. I think that is what mission tripping is all about. Landscaping is a needed service and it is one his many talents, but letting people know they are loved and cared about is what Jesus taught. About five years ago, the Lord tapped me on the shoulder and put a desire in my heart to go to Linefork. So now we go yearly together with the team and meet the Lord there as he always shows up in the most unexpected ways. The blessings for us have been beyond measure.

"Whoever wants to serve me must follow me, so that my servant will be with me where I am. And my Father will honor anyone who serves me" (John 12:26, GNB).

Jack has also been involved in a bicycle ministry at the CARE Center in Cornelius, NC. The Care Center is a Christian resource center founded by our church in a low-economic area.

The bicycle ministry is built on the concept of working towards a goal while being mentored by a Christian adult. The bike shop is located at the back of the Center where many bikes have been donated and lots of tools are to be found. Boys and girls come to the Center and select a bike they would like to have. They are then required to put in a certain number of hours working on the bike with a mentor. After achieving that goal, the bike is awarded to them in a small ceremony witnessed by their family. Jack has spent many hours working with these young people. How can one count the difference that might be making?

And so we see our Creator fitting the jigsaw pieces together. Jack's work of service to others here on earth and his pieces of the jigsaw puzzle were still being fitted together. The houses he has helped to build so people have a home for their family, the boys/men at the Sonshine Center, the boys/girls at the Bike Shop. How many lives has his life touched as the pieces fit together? There is no way to know. Only God knows how those pieces are fitting together. Some believe it will all be revealed to us when we get to Heaven. I am just sharing Jack's service and jigsaw pieces as a micro piece of God's plan. When one has a lifesaving experience, the world looks a bit different. Looking at a sure death and surviving brings GREAT thankfulness and a willingness to be used by God and be a part of putting God's jigsaw puzzle together according to his plan. Think about your life. How are you a piece of the puzzle that Jesus is putting together each day? Do you have many pieces that are being fitted with pieces of others? Who are you affecting maybe without knowing? Or on purpose with love in your heart and a deep desire to serve our Lord? It doesn't need to be huge acts as you know a smile can make someone's day. It is all in God's giant jigsaw puzzle plan with a pathway for each of His children.

"Each one, as a good manager, of God's different gifts, must use for the good of others the special gifts he has received from God" (I Peter 4:10, GNB).
I would like to add this final blessing we experienced this year. We were on a tour bustrip to Texas. About halfway through the

trip, by way of Joyce White and social media (I posted pictures of San Antonio on Facebook) we discovered Mandy's aunt and uncle, Joyce's brother, were on the bus tour with us. What a blessing! We kept this awesome secret between the four of us and the tour director as Jack did not want to become the focus for the rest of the trip. On the way home, the tour director allowed us to share this "small world" story with the group over the PA system. It was quite the moment. Applause broke out and then questions began. Some members of the group shared their miracle stories and people thanked us for sharing. Another miracle on our pathway!

The miracles continue in our lives and in yours. Be alert to see them as you walk with Jesus on the pathway God has for you. Ask the Holy Spirit to help you see them and keep your feet on the pathway created just for you. God will bless you and you will be so thankful.

"Your word is a lamp to guide me and a light for my path. I will keep my solemn promise to obey your instructions" (Psalms 119:105, GNB).

CHAPTER 13

Looking Back on God's Pathway

God's pathway for our lives to be where he has a plan for us can be perplexing or something we question while we are unsure of the pathway. Why am I moving? I love living right where I am, this city, this area. Or why can't I get out of this area I live in now? I want a job in another town/state/back home/away from home. Our pathway was certainly one of question for me time after time over the years. Jack and I were so happy that Jack was hired at Danville High School his first year out of college and our first year as newlyweds. We loved that little town and our friends there. We settled in after our wedding in the cutest mobile home you have ever seen. I figured we were in Danville for life. As two years of being citizens of Danville approached, we started talking about the search for our first house. It would be in Danville, of course. But Jack was showing a restlessness in his football job. His desire to be a head coach had him longing to learn more about coaching high school football. His thoughts would go back to our home high school, Highlands. If we moved to Ft. Thomas and he taught and coached at Highlands, the winner of several state football championships, he would increase his knowledge about successful coaching. The Lord opened that door, we packed a U-Haul truck and we moved. It just about broke my heart to leave Danville even though we were going "back home." I did love being close to my family again but even to this day, I think about how much I loved it there. During spring each year, I think about the awesome beauty of the many dogwood trees in full bloom. One of God's most beautiful trees. We had only been in Ft. Thomas for about four months when Jack had his first heart "event." We were glad to be close to his cardiologist that was practicing in Cincinnati at that time. We had been driving from Danville for his checkups. So now we needed him more and he was just minutes away. Maybe God put us here for a reason, even if I still longed for my sweet Danville. It was determined that Jack needed his aortic valve replaced. We went to Houston, Texas, where the surgery was performed by Dr. Denton Coley. Boy, was I glad to have family nearby when we returned home. Check off one for the God's life pathway. After five years in Ft. Thomas, Jack was hungry for that 1st high school head football coaching job. This path sent us to Georgetown, KY, where we lived for five years. Three at Scott County High School and two at Georgetown College as Dean of Men. During the time at Georgetown College, he filled in as the head football coach at Georgetown College. Working with the college young men was a new adventure and one he liked. But he decided he missed those high school boys and felt he could make more of a difference with them than the college young men. Along came the opportunity to go back to Highlands. So we moved and once again I was sadden to leave the city of Georgetown, the house I loved and our friends there. I thought surely this time was a permanent move. We would spend the rest of our lives back in our home town, close to family and with lifelong friends. We bought an eighty-something-year-old house just four doors and across the street from the elementary school. I had spent the night in that old house several times as one of my best friends, Margaret, grew up in that house.

I loved that squeaky old house even as a middle-schooler. Surely God brought us here forever. The fact that we were able to get that house was reason enough for me to believe this was our forever home. But I have learned God provides for us ALL the time, even if those times are temporary but we do not know it. We were there five years when Jack was asked to be the AD rather than the football coach. While that may seem like a natural step up the career ladder, Jack was not done working with those 15-18-year-olds. He declined the position and we moved onto London, Kentucky. What a great 22 years the Lord gave us there but the move was a difficult one for our children and me. I asked the Lord many times, often through heavy tears why we, especially our children, had to leave my hometown and my family. But as I look back now, it was part of the pathway God had for us. I started my very rewarding teaching career and Jack had a very successful coaching, teaching and counseling career there. Our children consider London their hometown. Our oldest son moved to NC with a restaurant chain and ultimately was hired with a NASCAR race team. Our 2nd son decided he wanted to do something with the building of the NASCAR racecars. He was a sophomore in high school and we enrolled him in the career/vocational track. Fortunately, we were in London/Laurel County as the technical training school is next to the high school. He would not have had that option in Ft. Thomas. Hmm. Another step in the pathway. He enjoyed welding and went on to obtain an Associate's degree. Both of our sons are still in the NASCAR industry and live in the Charlotte area. While we often think God has us on his pathway, we do not consider our children are on their own God directed pathway. I love the way God puts all the puzzle pieces together. We became familiar with NC and the Charlotte area and decided we would retire there someday to be close to our sons. Emily's family moves often for career purposes so we cannot follow her. We built our downsized home in 2005 but did not move until Jan. of 2010. A few months after building our house but not yet living there, Jack went to the Charlotte race by himself as I was working on our new house and our grand twins had a sporting event I wanted to see. Jack passed out in the racetrack parking lot due to a heart issue. There were some people there that God must have sent to help him. The jigsaw and pathway effect again. He was transported to the hospital and ended up having a new pacemaker with a defibrillator. I quickly became familiar with Carolinas Medical Center and their awesome heart program. Two years later we would be coming there for Jack's heart transplant with the donor passing in that hospital. One would think we would have gone to one of our state's transplant centers for the transplant but through a series of phone calls, we went to Carolina Medical Center to wait for Jack's heart. As we look back, God's pathway for us and our children has been truly amazing. We now have nine grandchildren. I am blessed by the fact each of their pathways includes Papa walking with them. Without Mandy's lifesaving donation of her heart, this would not be. Because we have had a look into death's cold stare a few times and experienced a lifesaving event, we have looked back to see the why of every move from town to town. What are the chances of a generous donor passing away in the same hospital where the perfect match is awaiting her fresh heart? That healthy heart would lovingly be carried across the hall and not need to come in by helicopter. This was the most surprising part of our reflection on our pathway. And it was so simple to see God's jigsaw-solving skills at work. Few people have the opportunity or take time to look back and see how God's pathway was the very best for them. We did.

I still have a longing for the beautiful places we have lived, the people that have touched our lives and the houses we have called home for a while. But above all of this is faith, faith that God always put us where he wanted us to be, doing what was best for us and our children. We always felt God's presence in our moves, knowing there was a plan we may not always understand or even like. What does God's pathway look like for you? Take some time to look back, pray and see how he has blessed you in each of your moves or in the same place. For you to do that is one of the purposes of this book: my reason for sharing my many experiences. I pray each of you will see the MIRACLES in your life along the PATHWAY God designed just for you.

Before our move to Georgetown, my dear friend, Gayle Davis, gave me the following saying, framed and surrounded with beautiful cutouts. I have treasured it as it is so true in my life. It has hung in every house I have lived in, except the first one. When those days of longing for another place hit me, I read it and smile and know God has blessed me in all my moves with many wonderful loving friends and special memories on His pathway for my life.

"You really never leave a place you love.
Part of it you take with you,
Leaving a part of you behind."
Author unknown